The Collected Works of

Langston Hughes

Volume 2

The Poems: 1941–1950

Projected Volumes in the Collected Works

The Poems: 1921–1940

The Poems: 1941–1950

The Poems: 1951–1967

The Novels: *Not without Laughter*
and *Tambourines to Glory*

The Plays to 1942: *Mulatto* to *The Sun Do Move*

The Gospel Plays, Operas, and Other
Late Dramatic Works

The Early Simple Stories

The Later Simple Stories

Essays on Art, Race, Politics, and World Affairs

Fight for Freedom and Other Writings on Civil Rights

Works for Children and Young Adults: Poetry,
Fiction, and Other Writing

Works for Children and Young Adults: Biographies

Autobiography: *The Big Sea*

Autobiography: *I Wonder As I Wander*

The Short Stories

The Translations: Federico García Lorca, Nicolás Guillén,
and Jacques Roumain

An Annotated Bibliography of the
Works of Langston Hughes

Publication of

The Collected Works of Langston Hughes

has been generously assisted by

Landon and Sarah Rowland

and

Morton and Estelle Sosland

The Collected Works of
Langston Hughes

Volume 2

The Poems: 1941–1950

Edited with an Introduction
by Arnold Rampersad

University of Missouri Press
Columbia and London

Library of Congress Cataloging-in-Publication Data

Hughes, Langston, 1902–1967.
   [Works. 2001]
   The collected works of Langston Hughes / edited with an introduction
      by Arnold Rampersad.
      p.   cm.
   Includes bibliographical references and indexes.
   ISBN 0-8262-1339-1 (v. 1 : alk. paper)—ISBN 0-8262-1340-5 (v. 2 : alk. paper)
   1. African Americans—Literary collections.   I. Rampersad, Arnold, II. Title.
PS3515.U274   2001
818'.5209—dc21   00-066601

⊗ This paper meets the requirements of the
American National Standard for Permanence of Paper
for Printed Library Materials, Z39.48, 1984.

Designer: Kristie Lee
Typesetter: BOOKCOMP, Inc.
Printer and binder: Thomson-Shore, Inc.
Typefaces: Galliard and Optima

Contents

Acknowledgments

The University of Missouri Press is grateful for assistance from the following individuals and institutions in locating and making available copies of the original editions used in the preparation of this edition: David Roessel; Anne Barker and June DeWeese, Ellis Library, University of Missouri–Columbia; Teresa Gipson, Miller Nichols Library, University of Missouri–Kansas City; Ruth Carruth and Patricia C. Willis, Beinecke Rare Book and Manuscript Library, Yale University; Ann Pathega, Washington University.

The *Collected Works* would not have been possible without the support and assistance of Patricia Powell, Chris Byrne, and Wendy Schmalz of Harold Ober Associates, representing the estate of Langston Hughes; of Judith Jones of Alfred A. Knopf, Inc.; and of Arnold Rampersad and Ramona Bass, co-executors of the estate of Langston Hughes.

Chronology

1902 James Langston Hughes is born February 1 in Joplin, Missouri, to James Nathaniel Hughes, a stenographer for a mining company, and Carrie Mercer Langston Hughes, a former government clerk.

1903 After his father immigrates to Mexico, Langston's mother takes him to Lawrence, Kansas, the home of Mary Langston, her twice-widowed mother. Mary Langston's first husband, Lewis Sheridan Leary, died fighting alongside John Brown at Harpers Ferry. Her second, Hughes's grandfather, was Charles Langston, a former abolitionist, Republican politician, and businessman.

1907 After a failed attempt at a reconciliation in Mexico, Langston and his mother return to Lawrence.

1909 Langston starts school in Topeka, Kansas, where he lives for a while with his mother before returning to his grandmother's home in Lawrence.

1915 Following Mary Langston's death, Hughes leaves Lawrence for Lincoln, Illinois, where his mother lives with her second husband, Homer Clark, and Homer Clark's young son by another union, Gwyn "Kit" Clark.

1916 Langston, elected class poet, graduates from the eighth grade. Moves to Cleveland, Ohio, and starts at Central High School there.

1918 Publishes early poems and short stories in his school's monthly magazine.

1919 Spends the summer in Toluca, Mexico, with his father.

1920 Graduates from Central High as class poet and editor of the school annual. Returns to Mexico to live with his father.

1921 In June, Hughes publishes "The Negro Speaks of Rivers" in *Crisis* magazine. In September, sponsored by his father, he enrolls at Columbia University in New York. Meets W. E. B. Du Bois, Jessie Fauset, and Countee Cullen.

1922   Unhappy at Columbia, Hughes withdraws from school and breaks with his father.

1923   Sailing in June to western Africa on the crew of a freighter, he visits Senegal, the Gold Coast, Nigeria, the Congo, and other countries.

1924   Spends several months in Paris working in the kitchen of a nightclub.

1925   Lives in Washington for a year with his mother. His poem "The Weary Blues" wins first prize in a contest sponsored by *Opportunity* magazine, which leads to a book contract with Knopf through Carl Van Vechten. Becomes friends with several other young artists of the Harlem Renaissance, including Zora Neale Hurston, Wallace Thurman, and Arna Bontemps.

1926   In January his first book, *The Weary Blues,* appears. He enrolls at historically black Lincoln University, Pennsylvania. In June, the *Nation* weekly magazine publishes his landmark essay "The Negro Artist and the Racial Mountain."

1927   Knopf publishes his second book of verse, *Fine Clothes to the Jew,* which is condemned in the black press. Hughes meets his powerful patron Mrs. Charlotte Osgood Mason. Travels in the South with Hurston, who is also taken up by Mrs. Mason.

1929   Hughes graduates from Lincoln University.

1930   Publishes his first novel, *Not without Laughter* (Knopf). Visits Cuba and meets fellow poet Nicolás Guillén. Hughes is dismissed by Mrs. Mason in a painful break made worse by false charges of dishonesty leveled by Hurston over their play *Mule Bone.*

1931   Demoralized, he travels to Haiti. Publishes work in the communist magazine *New Masses.* Supported by the Rosenwald Foundation, he tours the South taking his poetry to the people. In Alabama, he visits some of the Scottsboro Boys in prison. His brief collection of poems *Dear Lovely Death* is privately printed in Amenia, New York. Hughes and the illustrator Prentiss Taylor publish a verse pamphlet, *The Negro Mother.*

1932   With Taylor, he publishes *Scottsboro Limited,* a short play and four poems. From Knopf comes *The Dream Keeper,* a book of previously published poems selected for young people. Later, Macmillan brings out *Popo and Fifina,* a children's story about Haiti written with Arna Bontemps, his closest friend. In June, Hughes sails to Russia in a band of twenty-two young African Americans to make a film about race relations in the United States. After the project collapses, he lives for a year in the Soviet Union. Publishes his most radical verse, including "Good Morning Revolution" and "Goodbye Christ."

1933   Returns home at midyear via China and Japan. Supported by a patron, Noël Sullivan of San Francisco, Hughes spends a year in Carmel writing short stories.

1934   Knopf publishes his first short story collection, *The Ways of White Folks.* After labor unrest in California threatens his safety, he leaves for Mexico following news of his father's death.

1935   Spends several months in Mexico, mainly translating short stories by local leftist writers. Lives for some time with the photographer Henri Cartier-Bresson. Returning almost destitute to the United States, he joins his mother in Oberlin, Ohio. Visits New York for the Broadway production of his play *Mulatto* and clashes with its producer over changes in the script. Unhappy, he writes the poem "Let America Be America Again."

1936   Wins a Guggenheim Foundation fellowship for work on a novel but soon turns mainly to writing plays in association with the Karamu Theater in Cleveland. Karamu stages his farce *Little Ham* and his historical drama about Haiti, *Troubled Island.*

1937   Karamu stages *Joy to My Soul,* another comedy. In July, he visits Paris for the League of American Writers. He then travels to Spain, where he spends the rest of the year reporting on the civil war for the *Baltimore Afro-American.*

1938   In New York, Hughes founds the radical Harlem Suitcase Theater, which stages his agitprop play *Don't You Want to Be Free?* The leftist International Workers Order publishes *A New Song,* a pamphlet of radical verse. Karamu stages his play *Front Porch.* His mother dies.

1939 In Hollywood he writes the script for the movie *Way Down South,* which is criticized for stereotyping black life. Hughes goes for an extended stay in Carmel, California, again as the guest of Noël Sullivan.

1940 His autobiography *The Big Sea* appears (Knopf). He is picketed by a religious group for his poem "Goodbye Christ," which he publicly renounces.

1941 With a Rosenwald Fund fellowship for playwriting, he leaves California for Chicago, where he founds the Skyloft Players. Moves on to New York in December.

1942 Knopf publishes his book of verse *Shakespeare in Harlem.* The Skyloft Players stage his play *The Sun Do Move.* In the summer he resides at the Yaddo writers' and artists' colony, New York. Hughes also works as a writer in support of the war effort. In November he starts "Here to Yonder," a weekly column in the Chicago *Defender* newspaper.

1943 "Here to Yonder" introduces Jesse B. Semple, or Simple, a comic Harlem character who quickly becomes its most popular feature. Hughes publishes *Jim Crow's Last Stand* (Negro Publication Society of America), a pamphlet of verse about the struggle for civil rights.

1944 Comes under surveillance by the FBI because of his former radicalism.

1945 With Mercer Cook, translates and later publishes *Masters of the Dew* (Reynal and Hitchcock), a novel by Jacques Roumain of Haiti.

1947 His work as librettist with Kurt Weill and Elmer Rice on the Broadway musical play *Street Scene* brings Hughes a financial windfall. He vacations in Jamaica. Knopf publishes *Fields of Wonder,* his only book composed mainly of lyric poems on non-racial topics.

1948 Hughes is denounced (erroneously) as a communist in the U.S. Senate. He buys a townhouse in Harlem and moves in with his longtime friends Toy and Emerson Harper.

1949 Doubleday publishes *Poetry of the Negro, 1746–1949,* an anthology edited with Arna Bontemps. Also published are *One-Way Ticket* (Knopf), a book of poems, and *Cuba Libre: Poems of Nicolás Guillén* (Anderson and Ritchie), translated by Hughes and Ben Frederic Carruthers. Hughes teaches for three months at the University of Chicago Lab School for children. His opera about Haiti with William Grant Still, *Troubled Island,* is presented in New York.

1950 Another opera, *The Barrier,* with music by Jan Meyerowitz, is hailed in New York but later fails on Broadway. Simon and Schuster publishes *Simple Speaks His Mind,* the first of five books based on his newspaper columns.

1951 Hughes's book of poems about life in Harlem, *Montage of a Dream Deferred,* appears (Henry Holt).

1952 His second collection of short stories, *Laughing to Keep from Crying,* is published by Henry Holt. In its "First Book" series for children, Franklin Watts publishes Hughes's *The First Book of Negroes.*

1953 In March, forced to testify before Senator Joseph McCarthy's subcommittee on subversive activities, Hughes is exonerated after repudiating his past radicalism. *Simple Takes a Wife* appears.

1954 Mainly for young readers, he publishes *Famous Negro Americans* (Dodd, Mead) and *The First Book of Rhythms.*

1955 Publishes *The First Book of Jazz* and finishes *Famous Negro Music Makers* (Dodd, Mead). In November, Simon and Schuster publishes *The Sweet Flypaper of Life,* a narrative of Harlem with photographs by Roy DeCarava.

1956 Hughes's second volume of autobiography, *I Wonder As I Wander* (Rinehart), appears, as well as *A Pictorial History of the Negro* (Crown), coedited with Milton Meltzer, and *The First Book of the West Indies.*

1957 *Esther,* an opera with composer Jan Meyerowitz, has its premiere in Illinois. Rinehart publishes *Simple Stakes a Claim* as a novel.

Hughes's musical play *Simply Heavenly,* based on his Simple character, runs for several weeks off and then on Broadway. Hughes translates and publishes *Selected Poems of Gabriela Mistral* (Indiana University Press).

1958   *The Langston Hughes Reader* (George Braziller) also appears, as well as *The Book of Negro Folklore* (Dodd, Mead), coedited with Arna Bontemps, and another juvenile, *Famous Negro Heroes of America* (Dodd, Mead). John Day publishes a short novel, *Tambourines to Glory,* based on a Hughes gospel musical play.

1959   Hughes's *Selected Poems* published (Knopf).

1960   *The First Book of Africa* appears, along with *An African Treasury: Articles, Essays, Stories, Poems by Black Africans,* edited by Hughes (Crown).

1961   Inducted into the National Institute of Arts and Letters. Knopf publishes his book-length poem *Ask Your Mama: 12 Moods for Jazz. The Best of Simple,* drawn from the columns, appears (Hill and Wang). Hughes writes his gospel musical plays *Black Nativity* and *The Prodigal Son.* He visits Africa again.

1962   Begins a weekly column for the *New York Post.* Attends a writers' conference in Uganda. Publishes *Fight for Freedom: The Story of the NAACP,* commissioned by the organization.

1963   His third collection of short stories, *Something in Common,* appears from Hill and Wang. Indiana University Press publishes *Five Plays by Langston Hughes,* edited by Webster Smalley, as well as Hughes's anthology *Poems from Black Africa, Ethiopia, and Other Countries.*

1964   His musical play *Jericho–Jim Crow,* a tribute to the civil rights movement, is staged in Greenwich Village. Indiana University Press brings out his anthology *New Negro Poets: U.S.A.,* with a foreword by Gwendolyn Brooks.

1965   With novelists Paule Marshall and William Melvin Kelley, Hughes visits Europe for the U.S. State Department. His gospel play *The Prodigal Son* and his cantata with music by David Amram, *Let Us Remember,* are staged.

1966   After twenty-three years, Hughes ends his depiction of Simple in his Chicago *Defender* column. Publishes *The Book of Negro Humor* (Dodd, Mead). In a visit sponsored by the U.S. government, he is honored in Dakar, Senegal, at the First World Festival of Negro Arts.

1967 His *The Best Short Stories by Negro Writers: An Anthology from 1899 to the Present* (Little, Brown) includes the first published story by Alice Walker. On May 22, Hughes dies at New York Polyclinic Hospital in Manhattan from complications following prostate surgery. Later that year, two books appear: *The Panther and the Lash: Poems of Our Times* (Knopf) and, with Milton Meltzer, *Black Magic: A Pictorial History of the Negro in American Entertainment* (Prentice Hall).

The Collected Works of
Langston Hughes

Volume 2

The Poems: 1941–1950

Introduction

By 1941, at the age of thirty-nine, Langston Hughes was an accomplished and acknowledged American writer, with three volumes of verse, a novel, a book of short stories, and several plays and essays to his name. Although even a modicum of financial stability, much less prosperity, continued to elude him, he could find satisfaction in the respect and affection he commanded among a varied body of readers, and especially among both African Americans and Americans in general who loved lyric verse or were sympathetic to progressive causes.

Since the publication in 1921 of his first poem in a national magazine ("The Negro Speaks of Rivers" in W. E. B. Du Bois's *Crisis*), he had worked and developed steadily as an artist with a particular mission. He was a poet devoted to depicting and commenting on the African American cultural experience. He had boldly fused his command of traditional verse forms with impulses that sprang directly from black American culture, notably from the music called blues and jazz. He had also shown virtually from the start of his career that he was a poet of acute social consciousness and social conscience. In addition, Hughes was the author of many lyrical poems that revealed an artist responsive to the beauty but also the cruelty of nature, its final indifference to human life. Here, Langston Hughes was a poet of melancholy, at times almost to the point of existentialist gloom.

His first book, *The Weary Blues*, had been moderately well received by the general reading public when it appeared in 1926; among African Americans, however, it was an accomplishment that vaulted Hughes into the pantheon of the finest living black writers. His second volume, *Fine Clothes to the Jew*, almost got him expelled from that exclusive group when it appeared the following year; the poet's unprecedented devotion to the blues form and blues culture in general struck many middle-class readers as a violation of the art of poetry. In addition, the classic blues themes of love and loss, violence and despair, sexuality and frustration, which seemed to dominate the volume, appalled several reviewers, who chastised Hughes for exposing the seamy underbelly of black culture to public (white) scrutiny. But Hughes was not intimidated. In probably his finest essay, "The Negro Artist and the Racial Mountain," published in the *Nation* in June 1926, he had declared his right, and the right of every other younger black artist, to express himself and his racial feeling without fear or shame, and without regard to the feelings of blacks or whites. "We build our temples for tomorrow," Hughes had proclaimed, "strong as we know how, and we stand on top of the mountain, free within ourselves."[1]

In the 1930s, nevertheless, in response to a combination of harsh factors, Hughes effected a major change of focus in his poetry. The collapse of a vital relationship with a beloved patron, in addition to the national economic disaster that dealt a deathblow to the Harlem Renaissance as it dealt a harsh blow to many Americans and their dreams, drove him leftward as a political thinker and as an artist. Blues and jazz became less important than asserting the horrors of capitalism and the promise of international and interracial solidarity in a new system based on the abolition of class barriers. By 1932, when he arrived in Moscow as part of a group of young Americans, Hughes had committed himself to radical Marxism. His poems at that point in his career include the deliberately strident and iconoclastic "Good Morning Revolution" and "Goodbye Christ," "One More 'S' in the U.S.A." ("To make it Soviet"), and the equally excoriating "Letter to the Academy." When his publisher, Alfred A. Knopf, declined to publish such writing, Hughes turned to the leftist International Workers Order, which in 1938 brought out his most radical collection, *A New Song*.

By 1941, however, Hughes was ready for another basic reassessment of his ideas concerning both politics and poetry. Again the deciding factors were clear and urgent. There was the war raging in Europe that became an absolute concern for the American people in December 1941; patriotism, despite his resentment of Jim Crow, pulled Hughes

1. "The Negro Artist and the Racial Mountain," *Nation* 122 (June 23, 1926): 694.

toward aiding the national war effort and also toward the political center. In addition, he had come under critical fire for, in particular, the poem "Goodbye Christ." This poem includes a scathing reference to a popular evangelist, Aimee Semple McPherson, whose gospel church had a vigorous presence in southern California. After members of the sect disrupted a posh luncheon at which Hughes was engaged to speak about his new autobiography, *The Big Sea* (1940), the poet saw his career seriously threatened. His response was to surrender to the critics of the poem. Repudiating it, he attributed the writing of "Goodbye Christ" to the callousness of youth. "Having left the terrain of the 'radical at twenty' to approach the 'conservative at forty,' " and "desiring no longer to *épater le bourgeois,*" he declared, he "would not and could not write" such verse any more.[2]

At about the same time, he came under attack from the left for his role as a screenwriter in the musical film *Way Down South,* a sentimental melodrama about the Old South that was replete with stereotypes concerning black life on a Dixie plantation. In vain, and with a sense of deep frustration, Hughes protested that he had taken the job because his financial situation had become desperate. Only half jokingly, he decided at this point to return to safer themes—as he put it somewhere, he returned to writing about "Negroes, Nature, and Love." This was at best a half-truth. While he would write many poems in the following decade about blacks, nature, and love, Hughes would also redirect the political energy with which he had once endorsed radical socialism into the organized struggle against racial segregation. He would become a major bard of the embattled civil rights movement sustained mainly in the 1940s by the National Association for the Advancement of Colored People (NAACP) and its lawyers. (Later, Hughes would write an official history of the NAACP, *Fight for Freedom.*) Underscoring the absurdity of racial segregation or Jim Crow was the national expectation that blacks, although discriminated against in industry, educa-

2. "Statement Concerning Goodbye Christ," January 1, 1941, Langston Hughes Papers, Beinecke Rare Book and Manuscript Library, Yale University.

tion, politics, athletics, and indeed every significant aspect of American life, would join wholeheartedly in the fight against the Nazis and the Japanese in World War II. Hughes supported the war effort but also threw himself into the campaign for equal justice and opportunity for black Americans.

Nevertheless, in his determination to return his poetical career to firm ground, the first book of verse that Hughes published in this decade, *Shakespeare in Harlem* (Knopf, 1942), sidestepped politics in favor of blues and humor. Indeed, a small foreword by the author declared the volume to be "A book of light verse. Afro-Americana in the blues mood. . . . Blues, ballads, and reels to be read aloud, crooned, shouted, recited, and sung. Some with gestures, some not—as you like. None with a far-away voice." Hughes wished neither an undue solemnity nor traditional affectations about poetry to intrude into this renewal of his career-long celebration of African American life as seen from its "lower" strata.

In general, the response by reviewers indicated that Hughes had not yet convinced everyone that the blues was a fitting medium for formal poetry. As with the reception of *Fine Clothes to the Jew* in 1927, the responses of black critics were more negative than those of their white counterparts. *Opportunity*, the monthly magazine of the National Urban League, regretted that the volume was "concerned overmuch with the most uprooted, and hence demoralized Negro types." The leftist *Negro Quarterly* (its managing editor was Ralph Ellison) found the poems trivial and politically retrograde. In the *Chicago Bee* newspaper, the poet Frank Marshall Davis took the poems to be "slanted particularly for the Caucasian reader." However, in the mainstream press reviewers found much to praise. The *Christian Science Monitor* reported "a work of genuine talent and skillful artistry"; and the *Saturday Review of Literature* warned, "The careless reader might easily fall into the error of thinking that these delicate notes are funny or gay. It is only the skillful surface that is funny or gay; the heart of the matter is tragic. Rarely in our poetry do we find this subtle blending of tragedy and comedy. It is an exquisite art and a difficult one." Even the reviewer in the *New York Times Book Review*, who saw Hughes's art as distinctly limited intellectually and imaginatively, described nevertheless an "immensely sad, even hopeless" mood dominating the text.[3]

To some readers, clearly, the new poems raised old questions about the possible lack of intellectual and imaginative depth in Hughes's verse. "Various reviewers have accused me of never thinking at all," he commented in a response that mocked both himself and the society that insisted on treating him, because of the color of his skin, as an inferior. "The truth is that I do not think much, but occasionally I do think some. When I think I usually think this: Here I am in the world, poor, forty, and colored."[4]

Hughes's next collection of verse, *Jim Crow's Last Stand* (published not by Knopf but in pamphlet form by a decidedly marginal and leftist organization, the Negro Publication Society of America) captured a much angrier and more politically engaged poet. Here were poems such as "The Bitter River," about the lynching of two fourteen-year-old black boys in Mississippi, and "Good Morning, Stalingrad," an ode to the heroic defenders of the Russian city, an industrial center, against Hitler's armies; here Hughes came perhaps the closest he ever would to reviving his radical sympathies of the 1930s. Also notable from this period is "Freedom's Plow," although it was more an uplifting recitation piece than a work of complex poetic art ("America is a dream. / The poet says it was promises. / The people say it *is* promises—that will come true"). Reminiscent of his 1935 Depression anthem "Let America Be America Again," the poem would be followed in the next decade by other formal recitation pieces, such as "Freedom Train."

Another mode of verse—one can hardly call it poetry—developed by Hughes in these years reflected a democratic influence so extreme that it might be called excessively demotic. In this mode, the speaker of the poems typically appears to be barely educated, if educated at all, and

---

3. *Opportunity* 20 (July 1942): 219; *Chicago Bee*, April 5, 1942; *Christian Science Monitor*, April 1, 1942; *Saturday Review of Literature* 25 (April 25, 1942): 9; *New York Times Book Review*, March 22, 1942.
4. Note in "The Dark People of the Soviet," MS, n.d. [1942], Langston Hughes Papers, Yale.

certainly without any deep sense of, or interest in, the possibilities of cultivated poetic art. In "Total War," for example, banality is normal.

> The reason Dixie
> Is so mean today
> Is because it wasn't licked
> In the proper way. . . .
>
> I'm in favor of beating
> Hitler to his knees—
> Then beating him some more
> Until he hollers, *Please!*

Circulated in African American newspapers and deliberately intended for an even broader audience than was normal for Hughes, these pieces were a kind of counterpart in verse to his character Jesse B. Semple, or "Simple," a wryly comical black urban Everyman developed by the poet starting in 1943. Simple and his hilarious circle of friends and acquaintances appeared in the weekly column Hughes had started the previous year in the *Chicago Defender* and quickly became the most popular aspect of his creative writing. The columns, running over twenty years, eventually provided material for five books of sketches about Simple, starting with the popular *Simple Speaks His Mind* (1950). Also in this ultra-demotic vein, as if more contrived, and composed about the same time as *Jim Crow's Last Stand,* is Hughes's suite of poems "Madam to You." Here he created a brassy, irrepressible, and entirely memorable Harlem lady, Alberta K. Johnson, who smartly and tartly stands her ground against all comers. The title of the suite points to her insistence on being called "Madam" Alberta K. Johnson, as a mark of respect for her supreme (and unwittingly comic) individuality.

Demotic verse and satire were largely set aside in Hughes's next volume of verse, *Fields of Wonder* (1947). Here he returned to his old publishing house, Knopf, and submitted (willingly, no doubt) to its literary standards. Hughes not only set aside his demotic verse but also consciously crafted the first and only volume of his poetry that deliberately subordinated social and political causes in order to focus on the expression of his lyrical sensibility. While the two concluding sections of the book, "Stars over Harlem" and "Words Like Freedom," include poems that touch on the political, including a tribute to the Soviet army, lyricism is central here. Several of the poems are meditations, however brief and fragmentary, on nature; Hughes writes movingly about wind and rain, about the natural beauty of the mountains of Big Sur and the sea off Carmel in California. Not uncharacteristically in Hughes, nature also prompts disturbing feelings of loneliness, nihilism, and despair, as in poems such as "Border Line" and "Desire." Among the most memorable poems, combining gloom and racial feeling, a sense of the tragic along with Hughes's passionate regard for black music, is "Trumpet Player: 52nd Street":

> The Negro
> With the trumpet at his lips
> Whose jacket
> Has a *fine* one-button roll,
> Does not know
> Upon what riff the music slips
> Its hypodermic needle
> To his soul—

African American reviewers, often more conservative in their taste than their white counterparts, on the whole admired this volume of verse. The *New York Amsterdam News* reported that Hughes had "matured in his talents"; the *Baltimore Afro-American* declared that he had "rediscovered himself." However, communist publications such as *People's World* and *New Masses,* where Hughes had once been a darling, dismissed the work as empty and passionless. The mainstream press noted its appearance without enthusiasm.[5]

5. *New York Amsterdam News,* April 5, 1947; *Baltimore Afro-American,* April 12, 1947.

The year 1949 brought another volume of poetry published by Knopf, Hughes's *One-Way Ticket*. While *Fields of Wonder* had been consciously lyrical and antipolitical for the most part, *One-Way Ticket* was intended as a vigorous return to the urban folk material in which Hughes generally reveled. The first section comprised the twelve poems of his attractively comic "Madam to You" suite. Another poem, "The Ballad of Margie Polite," mockingly celebrated the woman whose rash reaction to a white policeman had led to the Harlem riot of 1943. More formal and hauntingly sensitive was "Song for Billie Holiday":

> What can purge my heart
>   Of the song
>   And the sadness?
> What can purge my heart
>   But the song
>   Of the sadness?
> What can purge my heart
>   Of the sadness
>   Of the song?

The final impression of the volume, nevertheless, is of the bouncy resilience of the poor black folk who stand at its center:

> You may hear me holler,
> You may see me cry—
> But I'll be dogged, sweet baby,
> If you gonna see me die.
>
> *Life is fine!*
> *Fine as wine!*
> *Life is fine!*

In contrast to the reception of *Fields of Wonder,* the new book antagonized reviewers in the black press. The same reviewer in the *Baltimore Afro-American* who had praised *Fields of Wonder,* the eminent literary scholar J. Saunders Redding, declared the new book "stale, flat and spiritless." The *Pittsburgh Courier* found proof here of what it had always suspected: Hughes lacked "about everything one expects in a poet." The mainstream press was somewhat more complimentary but only modestly so. One of these reviewers, David Daiches, writing in the *New York Herald Tribune,* called Hughes a "documentary" poet. While Daiches made it clear that being a documentary poet severely limited Hughes's sensitivity and intelligence, Hughes himself seemed to like the term and even began to apply it to himself. He was proud to be a "documentary" poet of African American life, setting down on paper the life and language of the people. Thus he gave in, perhaps wearily, to the old—and erroneous—suggestion that his work in the blues was largely stenographic, rather than the product of imaginative power.[6]

True, the sense among some critics that Hughes had become largely repetitive as a poet was not altogether unjustified. However, he was by no means finished as a writer—not while he linked his life and art as intimately as he did to the evolving and often volatile black culture mainly in Harlem. The district had exploded in the riot of 1943; crime was beginning to be a major issue, and illicit drugs began to infiltrate the culture and add to its growing disillusionment. Nevertheless, black people were resilient and life-affirming, and Hughes saw both sides of the cultural equation. Then, in 1948, an event involving his place among the people of Harlem seemed to set off in him a burst of inspiration that resulted in a remarkable volume of verse. In 1947, with his involvement as lyricist on the successful Broadway musical play *Street Scene,* written by Elmer Rice and with music by the renowned Kurt Weill, Hughes's financial situation improved dramatically (even as he faced right-wing hostility on the road, during his reading tours, that drained his energy). The main result of his financial windfall was his purchase of a townhouse in Harlem. This was the first home he ever owned, and the effect on him was exhilarating. Within days of taking up residence in 1948, Hughes made a major breakthrough in his poetic art.

6. *Baltimore Afro-American,* January 15, 1949; *Pittsburgh Courier,* February 5, 1949; *New York Herald Tribune,* January 9, 1949.

"I've completed a new book I wrote last week!" he marveled in a letter to his best friend and faithful correspondent, the writer Arna Bontemps. "No kidding—a full book-length poem in five sections called *Montage of a Dream Deferred*." The new poem, Hughes wrote excitedly, "is what you might call a precedent shattering opus—also could be known as a *tour de force*."[7] This book, with its entirely novel, deliberately disruptive bebop jazz rhythms that spoke to the troubled evolution of black culture in Harlem, would appear in 1951 (and thus may be found in Volume 3 of this edition of Hughes's poems). But its genesis in 1948 showed clearly that in this pivotal decade of his life, as he struggled to rehabilitate his life and career after the radical turbulence of the 1930s and the austerities and uncertainties of World War II, Langston Hughes was still devoted to his self-imposed life's task. He was still a writer whose deepest connection was to the African American people as part of the American republic, as well as to the development at every point of a poetic practice that reflected both the harsh realities and the artistic genius of their lives.

7. Hughes to Arna Bontemps, September 14, 1948, Langston Hughes Papers, Yale.

A Note on the Text

In presenting this three-volume edition of the poems of Langston Hughes as part of our *Collected Works of Langston Hughes,* we have chosen to highlight the individual books of verse prepared and published by Hughes, as opposed to a presentation of each poem in strict chronological order according to the date of its first publication, as in *The Collected Poems of Langston Hughes,* edited by Arnold Rampersad and David Roessel (New York: Knopf, 1994).

Thus, in Volume 2 (1941–1950) we offer the texts of four complete books of poems—*Shakespeare in Harlem* (1942), *Jim Crow's Last Stand* (1943), *Fields of Wonder* (1947), and *One-Way Ticket* (1949). In those few instances in which Hughes published the same poem (or an altered version) in two different volumes, we have included both printings of the poem in order to preserve the harmony of each volume.

"Uncollected" poems from 1941 to 1950, if they did not appear in a later book of verse prepared by Hughes, are presented in chronological order according to the date of their first publication. The texts of these "uncollected" poems come in general from Rampersad and Roessel, eds., *Collected Poems of Langston Hughes.* This volume, which presents the *last* published version of each poem, should be consulted for its bibliographical notes and other information.

Shakespeare in Harlem

(1942)

To Louise

Some of the poems in this book first appeared in *Poetry, The New Yorker, Esquire, Opportunity, Compass, Common Sense, Common Ground, The Carmel Pine Cone, Calendar: 1941.* To the editors of these magazines my thanks for permission to reprint.

A book of light verse. Afro-Americana in the blues mood. Poems syncopated and variegated in the colors of Harlem, Beale Street, West Dallas, and Chicago's South Side.

Blues, ballads, and reels to be read aloud, crooned, shouted, recited, and sung. Some with gestures, some not—as you like. None with a far-away voice.

Contents

Blues for Men

Death in Harlem

Mammy Songs

Ballads

Seven Moments of Love
An Un-Sonnet Sequence in Blues

Twilight Reverie

Here I set with a bitter old thought,
Something in my mind better I forgot.
Setting here thinking feeling sad.
Keep feeling like this I'm gonna start acting bad.
Gonna go get my pistol, I said forty-four—
Make you walk like a ghost if you bother me any more.
Gonna go get my pistol, I mean thirty-two,
And shoot all kinds o' shells into you.
Yal, here I set thinking—a bitter old thought
About two kinds o' pistols that I ain't got.
If I just had a Owl Head, old Owl Head would do,
Cause I'd take that Owl Head and fire on you.
But I ain't got no Owl Head and you done left town
And here I set thinking with a bitter old frown.
It's dark on this stoop, Lawd! The sun's gone down!

Supper Time

I look in the kettle, the kettle is dry.
Look in the bread box, nothing but a fly.
Turn on the light and look real good!
I would make a fire but there ain't no wood.
Look at that water dripping in the sink.
Listen at my heartbeats trying to think.
Listen at my footprints walking on the floor.
That place where your trunk was, ain't no trunk no more.
Place where your clothes hung's empty and bare.

Stay away if you want to, and see if I care!
If I had a fire I'd make me some tea
And set down and drink it, myself and me.
Lawd! I got to find me a woman for the WPA—
Cause if I don't they'll cut down my pay.

Bed Time

If this radio was good I'd get KDQ
And see what Count Basie's playing new.
If I had some money I'd stroll down the street
And jive some old broad I might meet.
Or if I wasn't so drowsy I'd look up Joe
And start a skin game with some chumps I know.
Or if it wasn't so late I might take a walk
And find somebody to kid and talk.
But since I got to get up at day,
I might as well put it on in the hay.
I can sleep *so* good with you away!
House is *so* quiet! . . . Listen at them mice.
Do I see a couple? Or did I count twice?
Dog-gone little mouses! I wish I was you!
A human gets lonesome if there ain't two.

Daybreak

Big Ben, I'm gonna bust you bang up side the wall!
Gonna hit you in the face and let you fall!
Alarm clock here ringing so damn loud
You must think you got to wake up a crowd!
You ain't got to wake up *no* body but me.
I'm the only one's got to pile out in the cold,
Make this early morning time to keep body and soul

Together in my big old down-home frame.
Say! You know I believe I'll change my name,
Change my color, change my ways,
And be a white man the rest of my days!
I wonder if white folks ever feel bad,
Getting up in the morning lonesome and sad?

Sunday

All day Sunday didn't even dress up.
Here by myself, I do as I please.
Don't have to go to church.
Don't have to go nowhere.
I wish I could tell you how much I *don't* care
How far you go, nor how long you stay—
Cause I'm sure enjoying myself today!
Set on the front porch as long as I please.
I wouldn't take you back if you come on your knees.
But this house is mighty quiet!
They ought to be some noise . . .
I'm gonna get up a poker game and invite the boys.
But the boys is all married! Pshaw!
Ain't that too bad?
They ought to be like me setting here—feeling glad!

Pay Day

This whole pay check's just for me.
Don't have to share it a-tall.
Don't have to hear nobody say,
"This week I need it all."
I'm gonna get it cashed,
Buy me a few things.

Ain't gonna pay a cent on that radio
Nor them two diamond rings
We bought for the wedding that's
Turned out so bad.
I'm gonna tell the furniture man to come
And take back all them things we had
That's been keeping my nose to the grindstone.
I never did like the installment plan
And I won't need no furniture living alone—
Cause I'm going back to rooming and be a free man.
I'm gonna rent me a cubby-hole with a single bed.
Ain't even gonna dream 'bout the womens I had.
Women's abominations! Just like a curse!
You was the best—but you *the worst*.

Letter

Dear Cassie: Yes, I got your letter.
It come last night.
What do you mean, why I didn't write?
What do you mean, just a little spat?
How did I know where you done gone at?
And even if I did, I was mad—
Left me by myself in a double bed.
Sure, I missed your trunk—but I didn't miss you.
Yal, come on back—I *know* you want to.
I might not forget and I might not forgive,
But you just as well be here where you due to live.
And if you think I been too mean before,
I'll try not to be that mean no more.
I can't get along with you, I can't get along without—
So let's just forget what this fuss was about.
Come on home and bake some corn bread,
And crochet a quilt for our double bed,

And wake me up gentle when the dawn appears
Cause that old alarm clock sho hurts my ears.
Here's five dollars, Cassie. Buy a ticket back.
I'll meet you at the bus station.
                    Your baby,
                    Jack.

Declarations

Evil

Looks like what drives me crazy
Don't have no effect on you—
But I'm gonna keep on at it
Till it drives you crazy, too.

Hope

Sometimes when I'm lonely,
Don't know why,
Keep thinkin' I won't be lonely
By and by.

Young Negro Girl

You are like a warm dark dusk
In the middle of June-time
When the first violets
Have almost forgotten their names
And the deep red roses bloom.

You are like a warm dark dusk
In the middle of June-time
Before the hot nights of summer
Burn white with stars.

Harlem Sweeties

Have you dug the spill
Of Sugar Hill?
Cast your gims
On this sepia thrill:
Brown sugar lassie,
Caramel treat,
Honey-gold baby
Sweet enough to eat.
Peach-skinned girlie,
Coffee and cream,
Chocolate darling
Out of a dream.
Walnut tinted
Or cocoa brown,
Pomegranate lipped
Pride of the town.
Rich cream colored
To plum-tinted black,
Feminine sweetness
In Harlem's no lack.
Glow of the quince
To blush of the rose.
Persimmon bronze
to cinnamon toes.
Blackberry cordial,
Virginia Dare wine—
All those sweet colors
Flavor Harlem of mine!
Walnut or cocoa,
Let me repeat:
Caramel, brown sugar,
A chocolate treat.
Molasses taffy,

Coffee and cream,
Licorice, clove, cinnamon
To a honey-brown dream.
Ginger, wine-gold,
Persimmon, blackberry,
All through the spectrum
Harlem girls vary—
So if you want to know beauty's
Rainbow-sweet thrill,
Stroll down luscious,
Delicious, *fine* Sugar Hill.

Little Lyric
(Of Great Importance)

I wish the rent
Was heaven sent.

Declaration

If I was a sea-lion
Swimming in the sea,
I would swim to China
And you never would see me.
   No!
   You never would
   See me.

If I was a rich boy
I'd buy myself a car,
Fill it up with gas
And drive so far, so far.
   Yes!

I would drive
So far.

Hard-hearted and unloving!
Hard-hearted and untrue!
If I was a bird I'd
Fly away from you.
   Yes, way
   Away
   From
   You.

Kid Sleepy

Listen, Kid Sleepy,
Don't you want to run around
To the other side of the house
Where the shade is?
It's sunny here
And your skin'll turn
A reddish-purple in the sun.

   Kid Sleepy said,
   I don't care.

Listen, Kid Sleepy,
Don't you want to get up
And go to work down-
Town somewhere
At six dollars a week
For lunches and car fare?

   Kid Sleepy said,
   I don't care.

Or would you rather,
Kid Sleepy, just
Stay here?

> *Rather just*
> *Stay here.*

Snob

If your reputation
In the community is good
Don't snub the other fellow—
It might be misunderstood—
Because a good reputation
Can commit suicide
By holding its head
Too far to one side.

Statement

Down on '33rd Street
They cut you
Every way they is.

Me and the Mule

My old mule,
He's got a grin on his face.
He's been a mule so long
He's forgot about his race.

I'm like that old mule—
Black
And don't give a damn!
So you got to take me
Like I am.

Present

De lady I work for
Told her husband
She wanted a
Robe o' love—
But de damn fool
Give her
A fur coat!

Yes,
He did!

Free Man

You can catch the wind,
You can catch the sea,
But you can't, pretty mama,
Ever catch me.

You can tame a rabbit,
Even tame a bear,
But you'll never, pretty mama,
Keep me caged up here.

If-ing

If I had some small change
I'd buy me a mule,
Get on that mule and
Ride like a fool.

If I had some greenbacks
I'd buy me a Packard,
Fill it up with gas and
Drive that baby backward.

If I had a million
I'd get me a plane
And everybody in America'd
Think I was insane.

But I ain't got a million,
Fact is, ain't got a dime—
So just by *if*-ing
I have a good time!

Aspiration

I wonder how it feels
To do cart wheels?
I sure would like
To know.

To walk a high wire
Is another desire,
In this world before
I go.

Blues for Men

Six-Bits Blues

Gimme six-bits' worth o' ticket
On a train that runs somewhere.
I say six-bits' worth o' ticket
On a train that runs somewhere.
I don't care where it's goin'
Just so it goes away from here.

Baby, gimme a little lovin',
But don't make it too long.
A little lovin', babe, but
Don't make it too long.
Make it short and sweet, your lovin',
So I can roll along.

I got to roll along!

Evenin' Air Blues

Folks, I come up North
Cause they told me de North was fine.
I come up North
Cause they told me de North was fine.
Been up here six months—
I'm about to lose my mind.

This mornin' for breakfast
I chawed de mornin' air.
This mornin' for breakfast
Chawed de mornin' air.

But this evenin' for supper,
I got evenin' air to spare.

Believe I'll do a little dancin'
Just to drive my blues away—
A little dancin'
To drive my blues away,
Cause when I'm dancin'
De blues forgets to stay.

But if you was to ask me
How de blues they come to be,
Says if you was to ask me
How de blues they come to be—
You wouldn't need to ask me:
Just look at me and see!

Out of Work

I walked de streets till
De shoes wore off my feet.
I done walked de streets till
De shoes wore off my feet.
Been lookin' for a job
So's that I could eat.

I couldn't find no job
So I went to de WPA.
Couldn't find no job
So I went to de WPA.
WPA man told me:
You got to live here a year and a day.

A year and a day, Lawd,
In this great big lonesome town!

A year and a day in this
Great big lonesome town!
I might starve for a year but
That extra day would get me down.

Did you ever try livin'
On two-bits minus two?
I say did you ever try livin'
On two-bits minus two?
Why don't you try it, folks,
And see what it would do to you?

Brief Encounter

I was lookin' for a sandwich, Judge,
Any old thing to eat.
I was walkin' down de street, Judge,
Lookin' for any old thing to eat—
When I come across that woman
That I didn't want to meet.

Judge, she is de woman
That put de miz on me.
She is de woman, Judge,
That put de miz on me.
If there's anybody on this earth, Judge,
I didn't want to see!

Fact that I hurt her, Judge,
De fact that she is dead,
Fact that I hurt her,
Fact that she is dead—
She was de wrongest thing, Judge,
That I ever had!

Morning After

I was so sick last night I
Didn't hardly know my mind.
So sick last night I
Didn't know my mind.
I drunk some bad licker that
Almost made me blind.

Had a dream last night I
Thought I was in hell.
I drempt last night I
Thought I was in hell.
Woke up and looked around me—
Babe, your mouth was open like a well.

I said, Baby! Baby!
Please don't snore so loud.
Baby! Please!
Please don't snore so loud.
You jest a little bit o' woman but you
Sound like a great big crowd.

Mississippi Levee

Been workin' on de levee,
Workin' like a tuck-tail dog.
Workin' on de levee
Like a tuck-tail dog.
When this flood is over,
Gonna sleep like a water-log.

Don't know why I build this levee
And de levee don't do no good.
Don't know why I build this levee

When de levee don't do no good.
I pack a million bags o' sand
But de water still makes a flood.

Levee, levee,
How high have you got to be?
Levee, levee,
How high have you got to be
To keep them cold muddy waters
From washin' over me?

In a Troubled Key

Do not sell me out, baby,
Please do not sell me out.
Do not sell me out, baby.
Do not sell me out.
I used to believe in you, baby,
Now I begins to doubt.

Still I can't help lovin' you,
Even though you do me wrong.
Says I can't help lovin' you
Though you do me wrong—
But my love might turn into a knife
Instead of to a song.

Only Woman Blues

I want to tell you 'bout that woman,
My used-to-be—
She was de meanest woman
I ever did see.

But she's de only
Woman that could mistreat me!

She could make me holler like a sissie,
Bark like a dog.
She could chase me up a tree
And then cut down de log—
Cause she's de only
Woman that could mistreat me.

She had long black hair,
Big black eyes,
Glory! Hallelujah!
Forgive them lies!
She's de only
Woman's gonna mistreat me.

I got her in Mississippi.
Took her to Alabam'.
When she left
I said, Go, hot damn!
You de last and only
Woman's gonna mistreat me.

Hey-Hey Blues

I can HEY on water
Same as I can HEY-HEY on beer.
HEY on water
Same as I can HEY-HEY on beer.
But if you gimme good corn whisky
I can HEY-HEY-HEY—and cheer!

If you can whip de blues, boy,
Then whip 'em all night long.

Boy, if you can whip de blues,
Then whip 'em all night long.
Just play 'em, perfesser,
Till you don't know right from wrong.

While you play 'em,
I will sing 'em, too.
And while you play 'em,
I'll sing 'em, too.
I don't care how you play 'em
I'll keep right up with you.

Cause I can HEY on water,
I said HEY-HEY on beer—
HEY on water
And HEY-HEY on beer—
But gimme good corn whisky
And I'll HEY-HEY-HEY—and cheer!

Yee-ee-e-who-ooo-oo-o!

Death in Harlem

Arabella Johnson and the Texas Kid
Went bustin into Dixie's bout one a.m.
The night was young—
But for a wise night-bird
The pickin's weren't bad on a 133rd.
The pickin's weren't bad—
His roll wasn't slim—
And Arabella Johnson had her
Hands on him.

At a big piano a little dark girl
Was playin jazz for a midnight world.
    Whip it, Miss Lucy!
    Aw, pick that rag!
    The Texas Kid's on a
    High-steppin jag.
A dumb little jigaboo from
Somewhere South.
A row of gold in his upper mouth.
A roll of bills in his left-hand pocket.
    Do it, Arabella!
    Honey baby, sock it!

Dancin close, and dancin sweet,
Down in a cellar back from the street,
In Dixie's place on 133rd
When the night is young—
For an old night-bird.
    Aw, pick it, Miss Lucy!

Jazz it slow!
It's good like that when you
Bass so low!

Folks at the tables drink and grin.
(Dixie makes his money on two-bit gin.)
Couples on the floor rock and shake.
(Dixie rents rooms at a buck a break.)
Loungers at the bar laugh out loud.
Everybody's happy. It's a spendin crowd—
Big time sports and girls who know
Dixie's ain't no place for a gang that's slow.
    Rock it, Arabella,
    Babe, you sho can go!

She says to the waiter,
Gin rickeys for two.
Says to Texas,
How'd a dance strike you?
Says to Lucy,
Play a long time, gal!
Says to the world,
Here's my sugar-daddy pal.
Whispers to Texas,
Boy, you're sweet!
She gurgles to Texas,
What you like to eat?
Spaghetti and gin, music and smoke,
And a woman cross the table when a man ain't broke—
When a man's won a fight in a big man's town—
    Aw, plunk it, Miss Lucy,
    Cause we dancin down!
A party of whites from Fifth Avenue
Came tippin into Dixie's to get a view.
Came tippin into Dixie's with smiles on their faces,

Knowin they can buy a dozen colored places.
Dixie grinned. Dixie bowed.
Dixie rubbed his hands and laughed out loud—
While a tall white woman
In an ermine cape
Looked at the blacks and
Thought of rape,
Looked at the blacks and
Thought of a rope,
Looked at the blacks and
Thought of flame,
And thought of something
Without a name.
   Aw, play it, Miss Lucy!
   Lawd!
   Ain't you shame?
Lucy was a-bassin it, boom, boom, boom,
When Arabella went to the LADIES' ROOM.
She left the Texas Kid settin by himself
All unsuspectin of the chippie on his left—
Her name was Bessie. She was brown and bold.
And she sat on her chair like a sweet jelly roll.
She cast her eyes on Texas, hollered,
Listen, boy,
While the music's playin let's
Spread some joy!

Now, Texas was a lover.
Bessie was, too.
They loved one another till
The music got through.
While Miss Lucy played it, boom, boom, boom,
And Arabella was busy in the LADIES' ROOM.
When she come out
She looked across the place—

And there was Bessie
Settin in her place!
(It was just as if somebody
Kicked her in the face.)

Arabella drew her pistol.
She uttered a cry.
Everybody dodged as
A ball passed by.
    A shot rang out.
Bessie pulled a knife,
But Arabella had her gun.
Stand back folkses, let us
Have our fun.
    And a shot rang out.
Some began to tremble and
Some began to scream.
Bessie stared at Bella
Like a woman in a dream
    As the shots rang out.
A white lady fainted.
A black woman cried.
But Bessie took a bullet to her
Heart and died
    As the shots rang out.
A whole slew of people
Went rushin for the door
And left poor Bessie bleedin
In that cellar on the floor
    When the shots rang out.
Then the place was empty,
No music didn't play,
And whoever loved Bessie was
Far away.

Take me,
Jesus, take me
Home today!

Oh, they nabbed Arabella
And drove her off to jail
Just as the sky in the
East turned pale
And night like a reefer-man
Slipped away
And the sun came up and
It was day—
But the Texas Kid,
With lovin in his head,
Picked up another woman and
Went to bed.

Wake

Tell all my mourners
To mourn in red—
Cause there ain' no sense
In my bein' dead.

Cabaret Girl Dies on Welfare Island

I hate to die this way with the quiet
Over everything like a shroud.
I'd rather die where the band's a-playin'
Noisy and loud.

Rather die the way I lived—
Drunk and rowdy and gay!

God! Why did you ever curse me
Makin' me die this way?

Sylvester's Dying Bed

I woke up this mornin'
'Bout half-past three.
All de womens in town
Was gathered round me.

Sweet gals was a-moanin',
"Sylvester's gonna die!"
And a hundred pretty mamas
Bowed their heads to cry.

I woke up little later
'Bout half-past fo',
De doctor 'n' undertaker's
Both at ma do'.

Black gals was a-beggin',
"You can't leave us here!"
Brown-skins cryin' "Daddy!
Honey! Baby! Don't go, dear!"

But I felt ma time's a-comin',
And I know'd I's dyin' fast.
I seed de River Jerden
A-creepin' muddy past—
But I's still Sweet Papa 'Vester,
Yes, sir! Long as life do last!

So I hollers, "Com'ere, babies,
Fo' to love yo' daddy right!"
And I reaches up to hug 'em—

When de Lawd put out de light.

Then everything was darkness
In a great . . . big . . . night.

Crossing

It was that lonely day, folks,
When I walked all by myself.
My friends was all around me
But it was just as if they'd left.
I went up on a mountain
In a high cold wind
And the coat that I was wearing
Was mosquito-netting thin.
Then I went down in the valley
And I crossed an icy stream
And the water I was crossing
Was no water in a dream
And the shoes that I was wearing
No protection for that stream.
Then I stood out on a prairie
And as far as I could see
Wasn't nobody on that prairie
That looked like me—
Cause it was that lonely day, folks,
When I walked all by myself
And my friends was right there with me
But was just as if they'd left.

Death Chant

They done took Cordelia
Out to stony lonesome ground.
Done took Cordelia
To stony lonesome,
Laid her down.
They done put Cordelia
Underneath that
Grassless mound.
      Ay-Lord!
          Ay-Lord!
              Ay-Lord!

She done left po' Buddy
To struggle by his self.
Yes, po' Buddy
Jones has done been left.
Now she's out in stony lonesome,
Lordy! Sleepin' by herself.
   Cordelia's
     In stony
       Lonesome
         Ground!

Mammy Songs

Southern Mammy Sings

Miss Gardner's in her garden.
Miss Yardman's in her yard.
Miss Michaelmas is at de mass
And I am gettin' tired!
  Lawd!
I am gettin' tired!

The nations they is fightin'
And the nations they done fit.
Sometimes I think that white folks
Ain't worth a little bit.
  No, m'am!
Ain't worth a little bit.

Last week they lynched a colored boy.
They hung him to a tree.
That colored boy ain't said a thing
But we all should be free.
  Yes, m'am!
We all should be free.

Not meanin' to be sassy
And not meanin' to be smart—
But sometimes I think that white folks
Just ain't got no heart.
  No, m'am!
Just ain't got no heart.

Share-Croppers

Just a herd of Negroes
Driven to the field,
Plowing, planting, hoeing,
To make the cotton yield.

When the cotton's picked
And the work is done
Boss man takes the money
And we get none,

Leaves us hungry, ragged
As we were before.
Year by year goes by
And we are nothing more

Than a herd of Negroes
Driven to the field—
Plowing life away
To make the cotton yield.

West Texas

Down in West Texas where de sun
Shines like de evil one
I had a woman
And her name
Was Joe.

Pickin' cotton in de field
Joe said I wonder how it would feel
For us to pack up
Our things
And go?

So we cranked up our old Ford
And we started down de road
And where
We was goin'
We didn't know—

Cause it's hard for a jigaboo
With a wife and children, too,
To make a livin'
Anywhere
Today.

But in West Texas where de sun
Shines like de evil one,
There ain't no reason
For a man
To stay!

Merry-Go-Round

Colored child at carnival:

Where is the Jim Crow section
On this merry-go-round,
Mister, cause I want to ride?
Down South where I come from
White and colored
Can't sit side by side.
Down South on the train
There's a Jim Crow car.
On the bus we're put in the back—
But there ain't no back
To a merry-go-round!
Where's the horse
For a kid that's black?

Ku Klux

They took me out
To some lonesome place.
They said, "Do you believe
In the great white race?"

I said, "Mister,
To tell you the truth,
I'd believe in anything
If you'd just turn me loose."

The white man said, "Boy,
Can it be
You're a-standin' there
A-sassin' me?"

They hit me in the head
And knocked me down.
And then they kicked me
On the ground.

A cracker said, "Nigger,
Look me in the face—
And tell me you believe in
The great white race."

Ballads

Ballad of the Sinner

I went down the road,
Dressed to kill—
Straight down the road
That leads to hell.

Mother warned me,
Warned me true.
Father warned me,
And Sister, too.

But I was bold,
Headstrong and wild.
I did not act like
My mother's child.

She begged me, please,
Stay on the right track.
But I was drinking licker,
Jitterbugging back,

Going down the road,
All dressed to kill—
The road that leads
Right straight to hell.

Pray for me, Mama!

Ballad of the Killer Boy

Bernice said she wanted
A diamond or two.
I said, Baby,
I'll get 'em for you.

Bernice said she wanted
A Packard car.
I said, Sugar,
Here you are.

Bernice said she needed
A bank full of cash.
I said, Honey,
That's nothing but trash.

I pulled that job
In the broad daylight.
The cashier trembled
And turned dead white.

He tried to guard
Other people's gold.
I said to hell
With your stingy soul!

There ain't no reason
To let you live!
I filled him full of holes
Like a sieve.

Now they've locked me
In the death house.
I'm gonna die!

Ask that woman—
She knows why.

Ballad of the Fortune-Teller

Madam could look in your hand—
Never seen you before—
And tell you more than
You'd want to know.

She could tell you about love,
And money, and such.
And she wouldn't
Charge you much.

A fellow came one day.
Madam took him in.
She treated him like
He was her kin.

Gave him money to gamble.
She gave him bread,
And let him sleep in her
Walnut bed.

Friends tried to tell her
Dave meant her no good.
Looks like she could've knowed it
If she only would.

He mistreated her terrible.
Beat her up bad.
Then went off and left her.
Stole all she had.

She tried to find out
What road he took.
There wasn't a trace
No way she looked.

That woman who could foresee
What *your* future meant,
Couldn't tell, to save her,
Where Dave went.

Ballad of the Girl Whose Name Is Mud

A girl with all that raising,
It's hard to understand
How she could get in trouble
With a no-good man.

The guy she gave her all to
Dropped her with a thud.
Now amongst decent people,
Dorothy's name is mud.

But nobody's seen her shed a tear,
Nor seen her hang her head.
Ain't even heard her murmur,
Lord, I wish I was dead!

No! The hussy's telling everybody
(Just as though it was no sin)
That if she had a chance
She'd do it agin!

Ballad of the Gypsy

I went to the Gypsy's.
Gypsy settin' all alone.
I said, Tell me, Gypsy,
When will my gal be home?

Gypsy said, Silver,
Put some silver in my hand
And I'll look into the future
And tell you all I can.

I crossed her palm with silver,
Then she started in to lie.
She said, Now, listen, Mister,
She'll be here by and by.

Aw, what a lie!

I been waitin' and a-waitin'
And she ain't come home yet.
Something musta happened
To make my gal forget.

Uh! I hates a lyin' Gypsy
Will take good money from you,
Tell you pretty stories
And take your money from you—

But if I was a Gypsy
I would take your money, too.

Ballad of the Pawnbroker

This gold watch and chain
That belonged to my father?
Two bucks on it?
Never mind! Don't bother.

How about this necklace?
Pure jade.
Chinese? . . . Hell, no!
It's union-made.

Can I get Ten on this suit
I bought two weeks ago?
I don't know why it looks
Worn so.

Feel the weight, Mr. Levy,
Of this silver bowl.
Stop hunting for the price tag!
It ain't stole.

O.K. You don't want it?
Then I'll go.
But a man's got to live,
You know.

Say! On the last thing I own,
Pawnbroker, old friend—
    Me!
    My self!
    Life!
What'll you lend?

Ballad of the Man Who's Gone

No money to bury him.
The relief gave Forty-Four.
The undertaker told 'em,
You'll need Sixty more

For a first-class funeral,
A hearse and two cars—
And maybe your friends'll
Send some flowers.

His wife took a paper
And went around.
Everybody that gave something
She put 'em down.

She raked up a Hundred
For her man that was dead.
His buddies brought flowers.
A funeral was had.

A minister preached—
And charged Five
To bless him dead
And praise him alive.

Now that he's buried—
God rest his soul—
Reckon there's no charge
For graveyard mold.

I wonder what makes
A funeral so high?
A poor man ain't got
No business to die.

Blues for Ladies

Down and Out

Baby, if you love me
Help me when I'm down and out.
If you love me, baby,
Help me when I'm down and out,
Cause I'm a po' gal
Nobody gives a damn about.

De credit man's done took ma clothes
And rent time's most nigh here.
Credit man's done took ma clothes.
Rent time's nearly here.
I'd like to buy a straightenin' comb,
An' I needs a dime fo' beer.

Oh, talk about yo' friendly friends
Bein' kind to you—
Yes, talk about yo' friendly friends
Bein' kind to you—
Just let yo'self git down and out
And then see what they'll do.

Love Again Blues

My life ain't nothin'
But a lot o' Gawd-knows-what.
I say my life ain't nothin'
But a lot o' Gawd-knows-what.
Just one thing after 'nother
Added to de trouble that I got.

When I got you I
Thought I had an angel-chile.
When I got you
Thought I had an angel-chile.
You turned out to be a devil
That mighty nigh drove me wild!

Tell me, tell me,
What makes love such an ache and pain?
Tell me what makes
Love such an ache and pain?
It takes you and it breaks you—
But you got to love again.

Midnight Chippie's Lament

I looked down 31st Street,
Not a soul but Lonesome Blue.
Down on 31st Street,
Nobody but Lonesome Blue.
I said come here, Lonesome,
And I will love you, too.

Feelin' so sad, Lawd,
Feelin' so sad and lone.
So sad, Lawd!
So sad and lone!
I said, please, Mr. Lonesome,
Don't leave me here alone.

Lonesome said, listen!
Said, listen! Hey!
Lonesome said, listen!
Woman, listen! Say!

Buy you two for a quarter
On State Street any day.

I said, Mr. Lonesome,
Don't ig me like you do.
Cripple Mr. Lonesome,
Please don't ig me like you do.
Lonesome said when a two-bit woman
Gives love away she's through.

Girls, don't stand on no corner
Cryin' to no Lonesome Blue!
I say don't stand on no corner
Cryin' to no Lonesome Blue!
Cry by yourself, girls,
So nobody can't low-rate you.

Widow Woman

Oh, that last long ride is a
Ride everybody must take.
Yes, that last long ride's a
Ride everybody must take.
And that final stop is a
Stop everybody must make.

When they put you in de ground and
They throw dirt in your face,
I say put you in de ground and
Throw dirt in your face,
That's one time, pretty papa,
You'll sure stay in your place.

You was a mighty lover and you
Ruled me many years.

A mighty lover, baby, cause you
Ruled me many years—
If I live to be a thousand
I'll never dry these tears.

I don't want nobody else and
Don't nobody else want me.
I say don't want nobody else
And don't nobody else want me—

Yet you never can tell when a
Woman like me is free!

Lenox Avenue

Shakespeare in Harlem

Hey ninny neigh!
And a hey nonny noe!
Where, oh, where
Did my sweet mama go?

Hey ninny neigh
With a tra-la-la-la!
They say your sweet mama
Went home to her ma.

Fired

Awake all night with loving
The bright day caught me
Unawares—asleep.

"Late to work again,"
The boss man said.
"You're fired!"

So I went on back to bed—
And dreamed the sweetest dreams,
With Caledonia's arm
Beneath my head.

Early Evening Quarrel

Where is that sugar, Hammond,
I sent you this morning to buy?
I say, where is that sugar
I sent you this morning to buy?
Coffee without sugar
Makes a good woman cry.

> *I ain't got no sugar, Hattie,*
> *I gambled your dime away.*
> *Ain't got no sugar, I*
> *Done gambled that dime away.*
> *But if you's a wise woman, Hattie,*
> *You ain't gonna have nothin to say.*

I ain't no wise woman, Hammond.
I am evil and mad.
Ain't no sense in a good woman
Bein treated so bad.

> *I don't treat you bad, Hattie,*
> *Neither does I treat you good.*
> *But I reckon I could treat you*
> *Worser if I would.*

Lawd, these things we women
Have to stand!
I wonder is there nowhere a
Do-right man?

Announcement

I had a gal,
She was driving alone,
Doing eighty
In a twenty-mile zone.

Had to pay her ticket.
It took all I had.
What makes a woman
Treat a man so bad?

Come to find out
(If I'd a-only knew it)
She had another joker
In my Buick!

So from now on,
I want the world to know,
That gal don't drive my
Car no more.

50-50

I'm all alone in this world, she said,
Ain't got nobody to share my bed,
Ain't got nobody to hold my hand—
The truth of the matter's
I ain't got no man.

Then Big Boy opened his mouth and said,
Trouble with you's
You ain't got no head!
If you had a head and used your mind

You could have *me* with you
All the time.

She answered, Babe, what must I do?

He said, Share your bed—
And your money, too.

Evil Morning

It must have been yesterday,
(I know it ain't today)
Must have been yesterday
I started feeling this a-way.

I feel so mean I could
Bite a nail in two.
But before I'd bite a nail
I'd pulverize you.

You're the cause
O' my feeling like a dog
With my feet in the mire
And my heart in a bog.

Uh! It sure is awful to
Feel bad two days straight.
Get out o' my sight be-
Fore it is too late!

Lover's Return

My old time daddy
Came back home last night.
His face was pale and
His eyes didn't look just right.

He says to me, "I'm
Comin' home to you—
So sick and lonesome
I don't know what to do."

> *Oh, men treats women*
> *Just like a pair o' shoes.*
> *You men treats women*
> *Like a pair o' shoes—*
> *You kicks 'em round and*
> *Does 'em like you choose.*

I looked at my daddy—
Lawd! and I wanted to cry.
He looked so thin—
Lawd! that I wanted to cry.
But de devil told me:
    Damn a lover
    Comes home to die!

Black Maria

Must be the Black Maria
That I see,
The Black Maria that I see—
But I hope it
Ain't comin' for me.

Hear that music playin' upstairs?
Aw, my heart is
Full of cares—
But that music playin' upstairs
Is for me.

Babe, did you ever
See de sun
Rise at dawnin' full of fun?
Says did you ever see de sun rise
Full of fun, full of fun?
Then you know a new day's
Done begun.

Black Maria passin' by
Leaves de sunrise in de sky—
And a new day,
Yes, a new day's
Done begun!

Reverie on the Harlem River

Did you ever go down to the river—
Two a.m. midnight by your self?
Sit down by the river
And wonder what you got left?

Did you ever think about your mother?
God bless her, dead and gone!
Did you ever think about your sweetheart
And wish she'd never been born?

Down on the Harlem River:
Two a.m.
Midnight!

By your self!
Lawd, I wish I could die—
But who would miss me if I left?

Love

Love is a wild wonder
And stars that sing,
Rocks that burst asunder
And mountains that take wing.

John Henry with his hammer
Makes a little spark.
That little spark is love
Dying in the dark.

Jim Crow's Last Stand

(1943)

Contents

The Black Man Speaks

I swear to the Lord
I still can't see
Why Democracy means
Everybody but me.

I swear to my soul
I can't understand
Why Freedom don't apply
To the black man.

I swear, by gum,
I really don't know
Why in the name of Liberty
You treat me so.

Down South you make me ride
In a Jim Crow car.
From Los Angeles to London
You spread your color bar.

Jim Crow Army,
And Navy, too—
Is Jim Crow Freedom the *best*
I can expect from you?

I simply raise these questions
Cause I want you to state
What kind of a world
We're fighting to create.

If we're fighting to create
A free world tomorrow,
Why not end *right now*
Old Jim Crow's sorrow?

Democracy

Democracy will not come
Today, this year,
Nor ever
Through compromise and fear.

I have as much right
As the other fellow has
To stand
On my two feet
And own the land.

I tire so of hearing people say,
Let things take their course.
Tomorrow is another day.
I do not need my freedom when I'm dead.
I cannot live on tomorrow's bread.

Freedom
Is a strong seed
Planted
In a great need.
Listen, America—
I live here, too.
I want freedom
Just as you.

Color

I would wear it
Like a banner for the proud—
Not like a shroud.
I would wear it

Like a song soaring high—
Not moan or cry.

Freedom

Some folks think
By burning books
They burn Freedom.

Some folks think
By imprisoning Nehru
They imprison Freedom.

Some folks think
By lynching a Negro
They lynch Freedom.

But Freedom
Stands up and laughs
In their faces
And says,

You'll never kill me!

Red Cross

The Angel of Mercy's
Got her wings in the mud,
And all because of
Negro blood.

Note to All Nazis Fascists and Klansmen

You delight,
So it would seem,
At making mince-meat
Of my dream.

If you keep on,
Before you're through,
I'll make mince-meat
Out of you.

How About It, Dixie

The President's Four Freedoms
Appeal to me.
I would like to see those Freedoms
Come to be.

If you believe
In the Four Freedoms, too,
Then share 'em with me—
Don't keep 'em all for you.

Show me that you mean
Democracy, please—
Cause from Bombay to Georgia
I'm beat to my knees.

You can't lock up Gandhi,
Club Roland Hayes,
Then make fine speeches
About Freedom's ways.

Looks like by now
Folks ought to know
It's hard to beat Hitler
Protecting Jim Crow.

Freedom's not just
To be won Over There.
It means Freedom at home, too—
Now—*right here!*

Blue Bayou

I went walkin'
By de blue bayou
And I saw de sun go down.

I thought about old Greeley
And I thought about Lou
And I saw de sun go down.

   White man
   Makes me work all day
   And I works too hard
   For too little pay—
   Then a white man
   Takes my woman away.

I'll kill old Greeley.
   De blue bayou
   Turns red as fire.
   Put the black man
   On a rope
   And pull him higher!

I saw de sun go down.

    Put him on a rope
    And pull him higher!
    De blue bayou's
    A pool of fire.

And I saw de sun go down,
    Down,
      Down!
Lawd, I saw de sun go down!

The Bitter River

(Dedicated to the memory of Charlie Lang and Ernest Green, each fourteen years old when lynched together beneath the Shubuta Bridge over the Chicasawhay River in Mississippi, October 12th, 1942.)

There is a bitter river
Flowing through the South.
Too long has the taste of its water
Been in my mouth.
There is a bitter river
Dark with filth and mud.
Too long has its evil poison
Poisoned my blood.
I've drunk of the bitter river
And its gall coats the red of my tongue,
Mixed with the blood of the lynched boys
From its iron bridge hung,
Mixed with the hopes that are drowned there
In the snake-like hiss of its stream
Where I drank of the bitter river
That strangled my dream:
The book studied—but useless,

Tools handled—but unused,
Knowledge acquired but thrown away,
Ambition battered and bruised.
Oh, water of the bitter river
With your taste of blood and clay,
You reflect no stars by night,
No sun by day.

The bitter river reflects no stars—
It gives back only the glint of steel bars
And dark bitter faces behind steel bars:
The Scottsboro boys behind steel bars,
Lewis Jones behind steel bars,
The voteless share-cropper behind steel bars,
The labor leader behind steel bars,
The soldier thrown from a Jim Crow bus behind steel bars,
The 15¢ mugger behind steel bars,
The girl who sells her body behind steel bars,
And my grandfather's back with its ladder of scars,
Long ago, long ago—the whip and steel bars—
The bitter river reflects no stars.

"Wait, be patient," you say.
"Your folks will have a better day."
But the swirl of the bitter river
Takes your words away.
"Work, education, patience
Will bring a better day."
The swirl of the bitter river
Carries your "patience" away.
"Disrupter! Agitator!
Trouble maker!" you say.
The swirl of the bitter river
Sweeps your lies away.

I did not ask for this river
Nor the taste of its bitter brew.
I was given its water
As a gift from you.
Yours has been the power
To force my back to the wall
And make me drink of the bitter cup
Mixed with blood and gall.

You have lynched my comrades
Where the iron bridge crosses the stream,
Underpaid me for my labor,
And spit in the face of my dream.
You forced me to the bitter river
With the hiss of its snake-like song—
Now your words no longer have meaning—
I have drunk at the river too long:
Dreamer of dreams to be broken,
Builder of hopes to be smashed,
Loser from an empty pocket
Of my meagre cash,
Bitter bearer of burdens
And singer of weary song,
I've drunk at the bitter river
With its filth and its mud too long.
Tired now of the bitter river,
Tired now of the pat on the back,
Tired now of the steel bars
Because my face is black,
I'm tired of segregation,
Tired of filth and mud,
I've drunk of the bitter river
And it's turned to steel in my blood.

Oh, tragic bitter river
Where the lynched boys hung,
The gall of your bitter water
Coats my tongue.
The blood of your bitter water
For me gives back no stars.
I'm tired of the bitter river:
Tired of the bars!

October 16

Perhaps today
You will remember John Brown.

John Brown
Who took his gun,
Took twenty-one companions
White and black,
Went to shoot your way to freedom
Where two rivers meet
And the hills of the
North
And the hills of the
South
Look slow at one another—
And died
For your sake.

Now that you are
Many years free,
And the echo of the Civil War
Has passed away.
And Brown himself
Has long been tried at law,

Hung by the neck,
And buried in the ground—
Since Harper's Ferry
Is alive with ghosts today,
Immortal raiders
Come again to town—

Perhaps
You will recall
John Brown.

Motherland

Dream of yesterday
And far-off long tomorrow:
Africa imprisoned
In her bitter sorrow.

Brothers

We are related—you and I.
You from the West Indies,
I from Kentucky.

We are kinsmen—you and I.
You from Africa,
I from these States.

We are brothers—you and I.

To Captain Mulzac

(Negro Skipper of *The Booker T. Washington*
Sailing with a Mixed Crew)

Dangerous
Are the western waters now,
And all the waters of the world.
Somehow,
Again mankind has lost its course,
Been driven off its way,
Down paths of death and darkness
Gone astray—
But there are those who still hold out
A chart and compass
For a better way—
And there are those who fight
To guard the harbor entrance
To a brighter day.

There are those, too, who for so long
Could not call their house, *their* house,
Nor their land, *their* land—
Formerly the beaten and the poor
Who did not own
The things they made, nor their own lives—
But stood, individual and alone,
Without power—
They have found their hour.
The clock is moving forward here—
But backward in the lands where fascist fear
Has taken hold,
And tyranny again is bold.

Yes, dangerous are the wide world's waters still,
Menaced by the will

Of those who would keep, or once more make
Slaves of men.
We Negroes have been slaves before.
We will *not* be again.
Alone, I know, no one is free.
But we have joined hands—
Black workers with white workers—
I, with you! You, with me!
Together we have launched a ship
That sails these dangerous seas—
But more than ship,
Our symbol of new liberties.
We've put a captain on that ship's bridge there,
A man, spare, swarthy, strong, foursquare—
But more than these,
He, too, a symbol of new liberties.

There is a crew of many races, too,
Many bloods—yet all of one blood still:
The blood of brotherhood,
Of courage, of good-will,
And deep determination geared to kill
The evil forces that would destroy
Our charts, our compass and bell-buoy
That guide us toward the harbor of the new world
We will to make—
The world where every ugly past mistake
Of hate and greed and race
Will have no place.

In union, you, White Man,
And I, Black Man,
Can be free.
More than ship then,
Captain Mulzac,

Is the BOOKER T.,
And more than captain
You who guide it on its way.
Your ship is mankind's deepest dream
Daring the sea—
Your ship is flagship
Of a newer day.

Let the winds rise then!
Let the great waves beat!
Your ship is Victory,
And not defeat.
Let the great waves rise
And the winds blow free!
   Your ship is
   Freedom,
   Brotherhood,
   Democracy!

Still Here

I've been scarred and battered.
My hopes the wind done scattered.
Snow has frize me, sun has baked me.
   Looks like between 'em
   They done tried to make me
Stop laughing, stop loving, stop living—
   But I don't care!
   I'm still here!

Visitors to the Black Belt

You can talk about
Across the railroad tracks—
But to me it's *here*
On this side of the tracks.

You can talk about
Up in Harlem—
But to me
It's *here* in Harlem.

You can say
Jazz on the South Side—
But to me
It's hell on the South Side:

　　Calumet Avenue's
　　Dingy houses
　　With no heat.

Who're you, outsider?
Ask me who am I.

Ballad of the Landlord

Landlord, Landlord,
My roof has sprung a leak.
Don't you 'member I told you about it
Way last week?

Landlord, Landlord,
These steps is broken down.
When you come up yourself
It's a wonder you don't fall down.

Ten bucks you say I owe you?
Ten bucks you say is due?
Well, that's Ten Bucks more'n I'll pay you
Till you fix this house up new.

What? You gonna get eviction orders?
You gonna cut off my heat?
You gonna take my furniture and
Throw it in the street?

Um-mhuh! You talking high and mighty.
Talk on—till you get through.
You ain't gonna be able to say a word
If I land my fist on you.

Police! Police!
Come and get this man!
He's trying to ruin the government
And overturn the land!

  Copper's whistle!
  Patrol bell!
  Arrest.
  Precinct Station.
  Iron cell.
  Headlines in press:

MAN THREATENS LANDLORD
TENANT HELD NO BAIL
JUDGE GIVES NEGRO 90 DAYS
IN COUNTY JAIL. . . .

Big Buddy

Big Buddy, Big Buddy,
Ain't you gonna stand by me?
Big Buddy, Big Buddy,
Ain't you gonna stand by me?
If I got to fight,
I'll fight like a man.
But say, Big Buddy,
Won't you lend a hand?
Ain't you gonna stand by me?

Big Buddy, Big Buddy,
Don't you hear this hammer ring?
Hey, Big Buddy,
Don't you hear this hammer ring?
I'm gonna split this rock
And split it wide!
When I split this rock,
Stand by my side.
Say, Big Buddy,
Don't you hear this hammer ring?

Ballad of Sam Solomon

Sam Solomon said,
You may call out the Klan
But you must've forgot
That a Negro is a MAN.
It was down in Miami
A few years ago.
Negroes never voted but
Sam said, It's time to go
To the polls election day

And make your choice known
Cause the vote is not restricted
To white folks alone.
The fact we never voted
In the past
Is something that surely
Ain't due to last.
Sam Solomon called on
Every colored man
To qualify and register
And take a stand
And be up and out and ready
On election day
To vote at the polls,
Come what may.
The crackers said, Sam,
If you carry this through,
Ain't no telling what
We'll do to you.
Sam Solomon answered,
I don't pay you no mind.
The crackers said, Boy,
Are you deaf, dumb, and blind?
Sam Solomon said, I'm
Neither one nor the other—
But we intend to vote
On election day, brother.
The crackers said, Sam,
Are you a fool or a dunce?
Sam Solomon said, A MAN
Can't die but once.
They called out the Klan.
They had a parade.
But Sam Solomon
Was not afraid.

On election day
He led his colored delegation
To take their rightful part
In the voting of a nation.
The crackers thought
The Ku Klux was tough—
But the Negroes in Miami
Called their bluff.
Sam Solomon said,
Go *get* out your Klan—
But you must've forgotten
A Negro is a MAN.

Note on Commercial Theatre

You've taken my blues and gone—
You sing 'em on Broadway
And you sing 'em in Hollywood Bowl,
And you mixed 'em up with symphonies
And you fixed 'em
So they don't sound like me.

Yep, you done taken my blues and gone.

You also took my spirituals and gone.
You put me in Macbeth
And all kinds of Swing Mikados
And in everything but what's about me—
But someday somebody'll
Stand up and talk about me,
And write about me—
Black and beautiful—
And sing about me,
And put on plays about me!

I reckon it'll be
Me myself!

It'll be me.

Daybreak in Alabama

When I get to be a colored composer
I'm gonna write me some music about
Daybreak in Alabama
And I'm gonna put the purtiest songs in it
Rising out of the ground like a swamp mist
And falling out of heaven like soft dew
I'm gonna put some tall tall trees in it
And the scent of pine needles
And the smell of red clay after rain
And long red necks
And poppy colored faces
And big brown arms
And the field daisy eyes
Of black and white black white black people
And I'm gonna put white hands
And black hands and brown and yellow hands
And red clay earth hands in it
Touching everybody with kind fingers
Touching each other natural as dew
In that dawn of music when I
Get to be a colored composer
And write about daybreak
In Alabama.

Me and My Song

Black
As the gentle night
Black
As the kind and quiet night
Black
As the deep productive earth
Body
Out of Africa
Strong and black
As iron
First smelted in
Africa
Song
Out of Africa
Deep and mellow song
Rich
As the black earth
Strong
As black iron
Kind
As the black night
My song
From the dark lips
Of Africa
Deep
As the rich earth
Beautiful
As the black night
Strong
As the first iron
Black
Out of Africa

Me and my
Song

Good Morning, Stalingrad

Goodmorning, Stalingrad!
Lots of folks who don't like you
Had give you up for dead.
But you ain't dead!

Goodmorning, Stalingrad!
Where I live down in Dixie
Things is bad—
But they're not so bad
I still can't say,
Goodmorning, Stalingrad!
And I'm not so dumb
I still don't know
That as long as your red star
Lights the sky,
We won't die.

Goodmorning, Stalingrad!
You're half a world away or more
But when your guns roar,
They roar for me—
And for everybody
Who wants to be free.

Goodmorning, Stalingrad!
Some folks try to tell me down this way
That you're our ally just for today.
That may be so—for those who want it so,
But as for me—you're my ally
Until we *all* are free.

Goodmorning, Stalingrad!
When crooks and klansmen
Lift their heads and things is bad,
I can look way across the sea
And see where simple working folks like me
Lift their heads, too, with gun in hand
To drive the fascists from the land.
You've stood between us well,
Stalingrad!
The folks who hate you'd
Done give you up for dead—
They were glad.

But you ain't dead!

And you won't be
As long as I am you
And you are me—
For you have allies everywhere,
All over the world, who care.
And they
Are with you more
Than just today.

Listen! I don't own no radio—
Can't send no messages through the air.
But I reckon you can hear me,
Anyhow, away off there.
And I know you know
I mean it when I say,
(Maybe in a whisper
To keep the Klan away)
Goodmorning, Stalingrad!

I'm glad
You ain't dead!

GOODMORNING, STALINGRAD!

Jim Crow's Last Stand

There was an old Crow by the name of Jim.
The Crackers were in love with him.
They liked him so well they couldn't stand
To see Jim Crow get out of hand.
But something happened, Jim's feathers fell.
Now that Crow's begun to look like hell.

   DECEMBER 7, 1941:

Pearl Harbor put Jim Crow on the run.
That Crow can't fight for Democracy
And be the same old Crow he used to be—
Although right now, even yet today,
He still tries to act in the same old way.
But India and China and Harlem, too,
Have made up their minds Jim Crow is through.
Nehru said, before he went to jail,
Catch that Jim Crow bird, pull the feathers out his tail!
Marion Anderson said to the DAR,
I'll sing for you—but drop that color bar.
Paul Robeson said, out in Kansas City,
To Jim Crow my people is a pity.
Mrs. Bethune told Martin Dies,
You ain't telling nothing but your Jim Crow lies—
If you want to get old Hitler's goat,
Abolish poll tax so folks can vote.
Joe Louis said, We gonna win this war
Cause the good Lord knows what *we're* fighting for!

DECEMBER 7, 1941:

When Dorie Miller took gun in hand—
Jim Crow started his last stand.
Our battle yet is far from won
But when it is, Jim Crow'll be done.
We gonna bury that son-of-a-gun!

Fields of Wonder

(1947)

To Arna and Alberta Bontemps

Acknowledgment

The author wishes to thank the editors of *Poetry*, the *Saturday Evening Post*, *Harper's Bazaar*, *Opportunity*, the *Carmel Pine Cone*, *New York Herald Tribune Books*, the *Kansas Magazine*, the *Crisis*, The Beechhurst Press, Inc., and the *Poetry Quarterly* for permission to reprint previously published poems.

Contents

Fields of Wonder

Heaven

Heaven is
The place where
Happiness is
Everywhere.

Animals
And birds sing—
As does
Everything.

To each stone,
"How-do-you-do?"
Stone answers back,
"Well! And you?"

Snail

Little snail,
Dreaming you go.
Weather and rose
Is all you know.

Weather and rose
Is all you see,
Drinking
The dewdrop's
Mystery.

Big Sur

Great lonely hills.
Great mountains.
Mighty touchstones of song.

Moonlight Night: Carmel

Tonight the waves march
In long ranks
Cutting the darkness
With their silver shanks,
Cutting the darkness
And kissing the moon
And beating the land's
Edge into a swoon.

Snake

He glides so swiftly
Back into the grass—
Gives me the courtesy of road
To let me pass,
That I am half ashamed
To seek a stone
To kill him.

New Moon

There's a new young moon
Riding the hills tonight.

There's a sprightly young moon
Exploring the clouds.

There's a half-shy young moon
Veiling her face like a virgin
Waiting for a lover.

Birth

Oh, fields of wonder
Out of which
Stars are born,
And moon and sun
And me as well,
Like stroke
Of lightning
In the night
Some mark
To make
Some word
To tell.

Border Line

Border Line

I used to wonder
About living and dying—
I think the difference lies
Between tears and crying.

I used to wonder
About here and there—
I think the distance
Is nowhere.

Night: Four Songs

Night of the two moons
And the seventeen stars,
Night of the day before yesterday
And the day after tomorrow,
Night of the four songs unsung:
 Sorrow! Sorrow!
 Sorrow! Sorrow!

Dustbowl

The land
Wants me to come back
To a handful of dust in autumn,
To a raindrop
In the palm of my hand

In spring.

The land
Wants me to come back
To a broken song in October,
To a snowbird on the wing.

The land
Wants me
To come back.

Burden

It is not weariness
That bows me down,
But sudden nearness
To song without sound.

One

Lonely
As the wind
On the Lincoln
Prairies.

Lonely
As a bottle of likker
On a table
All by itself.

Beale Street

The dream is vague
And all confused
With dice and women
And jazz and booze.

The dream is vague,
Without a name,
Yet warm and wavering
And sharp as flame.

The loss
Of the dream
Leaves nothing
The same.

Gifts

To some people
Love is given.
To others—
Only heaven.

Circles

The circles spin round
And the circles spin round
And meet their own tail.

Seasons come, seasons go,
The years build their bars
Till we're in jail.

Like a squirrel in a cage—
For the jail is round—
We sometimes find
Ourselves upside down.

Grave Yard

Here is that sleeping place,
Long resting place,
No stretching place,
That never-get-up-no-more
    Place
    Is here.

Convent

Tell me,
Is there peace
Behind your high stone walls—
Peace
Where no worldly duty calls—
Or does some strange
Insistence beckon
With a challenge
That appalls?

Poppy Flower

A wild poppy-flower
Withered and died.

The day-people laughed—
But the night-people cried.

A wild poppy-flower
Withered and died.

Gypsy Melodies

Songs that break
And scatter
Out of the moon:
Rockets of joy
Dimmed too soon.

Montmartre

  Pigalle:
  A neon rose
In a champagne bottle.
  At dawn
  The petals
  Fall.

Fragments

Whispers
Of springtime.

Death in the night.

A song
With too many
Tunes.

Desert

Anybody
Better than
Nobody.

In the barren dusk
Even the snake
That spirals
Terror on the sand—

Better than nobody
In this lonely
Land.

End

There are
No clocks on the wall,
And no time,
No shadows that move
From dawn to dusk
Across the floor.

There is neither light
Nor dark
Outside the door.

There is no door!

Heart on the Wall

Heart

Pierrot
Took his heart
And hung it
On a wayside wall.

He said,
"Look, Passers-by,
Here is my heart!"

But no one was curious.
No one cared at all
That there hung
Pierrot's heart
On the public wall.

So Pierrot
Took his heart
And hid it
Far away.

Now people wonder
Where his heart is
Today.

Remembrance

To wander through this living world
And leave uncut the roses
Is to remember fragrance where
The flower no scent encloses.

Havana Dreams

The dream is a cocktail at Sloppy Joe's—
(Maybe—nobody knows.)

The dream is the road to Batabano.
(But nobody knows if that is so.)

Perhaps the dream is only her face—
Perhaps it's a fan of silver lace—
Or maybe the dream's a Vedado rose—
(*Quien sabe?* Who really knows?)

Girl

She lived in sinful happiness
And died in pain.
She danced in sunshine
And laughed in rain.

She went one summer morning
When flowers spread the plain,
But she told everybody
She was coming back again.

Folks made a coffin
And hid her deep in earth.
Seems like she said:
My body
Brings new birth.

For sure there grew flowers
And tall young trees
And sturdy weeds and grasses
To sway in the breeze.

And sure she lived
In growing things
With no pain
To laugh in sunshine
And dance in rain.

For Dead Mimes

O white-faced mimes,
May rose leaves
Cover you
Like crimson
Snow.

And may Pierrette,
The faithful,
Rest forever
With Pierrot.

Silver Rain

In Time of Silver Rain

In time of silver rain
The earth
Puts forth new life again,
Green grasses grow
And flowers lift their heads,
And over all the plain
The wonder spreads
 Of life,
 Of life,
 Of life!

In time of silver rain
The butterflies
Lift silken wings
To catch a rainbow cry,
And trees put forth
New leaves to sing
In joy beneath the sky
As down the roadway
Passing boys and girls
Go singing, too,
In time of silver rain
 When spring
 And life
 Are new.

Fulfilment

The earth-meaning
Like the sky-meaning
Was fulfilled.

We got up
And went to the river,
Touched silver water,
Laughed and bathed
In the sunshine.

Day
Became a bright ball of light
For us to play with,
Sunset
A yellow curtain,
Night
A velvet screen.

The moon,
Like an old grandmother,
Blessed us with a kiss
And sleep
Took us both in
Laughing.

Night Song

In the dark
Before the tall
Moon came,
Little short
Dusk

Was walking
Along.

In the dark
Before the tall
Moon came,
Little short
Dusk
Was singing
A song.

In the dark
Before the tall
Moon came,
A lady named
Day
Fainted away
In the
Dark.

Silence

I catch the pattern
Of your silence
Before you speak.

I do not need
To hear a word.

In your silence
Every tone I seek
Is heard.

Carolina Cabin

There's hanging moss
And holly
And tall straight pine
About this little cabin
In the wood.

Inside
A crackling fire,
Warm red wine,
And youth and life
And laughter
That is good.

Outside
The world is gloomy,
The winds of winter cold,
As down the road
A wandering poet
Must roam.

But here there's peace
And laughter
And love's old story told—
Where two people
Make a home.

Songs

I sat there singing her
Songs in the dark.

She said,
I do not understand
The words.

I said,
There are
No words.

Sleep

When the lips
And the body
Are done
She seeks your hand,
Touches it,
And sleep comes,
Without wonder
And without dreams,
When the lips
And the body
Are done.

Desire

Desire

Desire to us
Was like a double death,
Swift dying
Of our mingled breath,
Evaporation
Of an unknown strange perfume
Between us quickly
In a naked
Room.

Dream

Last night I dreamt
This most strange dream,
And everywhere I saw
What did not seem could ever be:

You were not there with me!

Awake,
I turned
And touched you
Asleep,
Face to the wall.

I said,
How dreams
Can lie!

But you were not there at all!

Juliet

There are wonder
And pain
And terror,
And sick silly songs
Of sorrow,
And the marrow
Of the bone
Of life
Smeared across
Her mouth.

The road
From Verona
To Mantova
Is dusty
With the drought.

Man

I was a boy then.
I did not understand—
I thought that friendship lay
In the grip of hand to hand.
I thought that love must be
Her body close to mine.
I thought that drunkenness
Was real—
In wine.

But I was a boy then,
I didn't understand
The things a young lad

Learns so soon
When he's
A man.

Tearless

Vagabonds

We are the desperate
Who do not care,
The hungry
Who have nowhere
To eat,
No place to sleep,
The tearless
Who cannot
Weep.

Luck

Sometimes a few scraps fall
From the tables of joy.
Sometimes a bone
Is flung.

Exits

The sea is deep,
A knife is sharp,
And a poison acid burns—
But they all bring rest,
They all bring peace
For which the tired
Soul yearns.
They all bring rest

In a nothingness
From where
No soul returns.

Walls

Four walls can hold
So much pain,
Four walls that shield
From the wind and rain.

Four walls can shelter
So much sorrow
Garnered from yesterday
And held for tomorrow.

Chippy

Rose of neon darkness,
Rose of the sharp-thorned stem
And the rouge-bright petals,
Rose of nothing but yesterdays
Too bitter to remember—
Little dollar rose
Of the bar stools
Facing a two-bit
December.

Dancers

Stealing from the night
A few
Desperate hours
Of pleasure.

Stealing from death
A few
Desperate days
Of life.

Grief

Eyes
That are frozen
From not crying.

Heart
That knows
No way of dying.

Prayer

Gather up
In the arms of your pity
The sick, the depraved,
The desperate, the tired,
All the scum
Of our weary city
Gather up
In the arms of your pity.
Gather up

In the arms of your love—
Those who expect
No love from above.

Mortal Storm

A House in Taos

Rain

Thunder of the Rain God:
  And we three
  Smitten by beauty.

Thunder of the Rain God:
  And we three
  Weary, weary.

Thunder of the Rain God:
  And you, she, and I
  Waiting for nothingness.

Do you understand the stillness
  Of this house
  In Taos
Under the thunder of the Rain God?

Sun

That there should be a barren garden
About this house in Taos
Is not so strange,
But that there should be three barren hearts
In this one house in Taos—
Who carries ugly things to show the sun?

Moon

Did you ask for the beaten brass of the moon?

We can buy lovely things with money,
You, she, and I,
Yet you seek,
As though you could keep,
This unbought loveliness of moon.

Wind

Touch our bodies, wind.
Our bodies are separate, individual things.
Touch our bodies, wind,
But blow quickly
Through the red, white, yellow skins
Of our bodies
To the terrible snarl,
Not mine,
Not yours,
Not hers,
But all one snarl of souls.
Blow quickly, wind,
Before we run back
Into the windlessness—
With our bodies—
Into the windlessness
Of our house in Taos.

Old Sailor

He has been
Many places
In ships
That cross the sea,
Has studied varied faces,
Has tasted mystery,
In Oriental cities

Has breasted
Monstrous pities
And to all
Fleshly pleasures
Known the key.
Now,
Paralyzed,
He suns himself
In charity's poor chair—
And dreams
That women he has left
Lament him
Everywhere.

Genius Child

This is a song for the genius child.
Sing it softly, for the song is wild.
Sing it softly as ever you can—
Lest the song get out of hand.

Nobody loves a genius child.

Can you love an eagle,
Tame or wild?
Can you love an eagle,
Wild or tame?
Can you love a monster
Of frightening name?

Nobody loves a genius child.

Kill him—and let his soul run wild!

Dream Dust

Gather out of star-dust
   Earth-dust,
   Cloud-dust,
   Storm-dust,
And splinters of hail,
One handful of dream-dust
   Not for sale.

Strange Hurt

In times of stormy weather
She felt queer pain
That said,
"You'll find rain better
Than shelter from the rain."

Days filled with fiery sunshine
Strange hurt she knew
That made
Her seek the burning sunlight
Rather than the shade.

In months of snowy winter
When cozy houses hold,
She'd break down doors
To wander naked
In the cold.

Little Song

Lonely people
In the lonely night
Grab a lonely dream
And hold it tight.

Lonely people
In the lonely day
Work to salt
Their dream away.

Personal

In an envelope marked:
    Personal
God addressed me a letter.
In an envelope marked:
    Personal
I have given my answer.

Jaime

He sits on a hill
And beats a drum
For the great earth spirits
That never come.

He sits on a hill
Looking out to sea
Toward a mirage-land
That will never be.

Faithful One

Though I go drunken
To her door,
I'm ever so sure
She'll let me in.

Though I wander and stray
And wound her sore,
She'll open the latch
When I come again.

No matter what
I do or say,
She waits for me
At the end of day.

Sailing Date

Twisted and strange
Their lives
With bitter range
From salt sea water
To a whiskey shore.

On sailing date,
Old seamen
Who've weathered
A thousand storms,
Two wars
And submarines
From here to there,
Go up the gangplank
To the Nevermore—
Perhaps—

Or just another
Trip.

Why care?
It's sailing date.
Their captain's
There.

There

Where death
Stretches its wide horizons
And the sun gallops no more
Across the sky,
There where nothing
Is all,
I,
Who am nobody,
Will become Infinity,
Even perhaps
Divinity.

Stars over Harlem

Trumpet Player: 52nd Street

The Negro
With the trumpet at his lips
Has dark moons of weariness
Beneath his eyes
Where the smoldering memory
Of slave ships
Blazed to the crack of whips
About his thighs.

The Negro
With the trumpet at his lips
Has a head of vibrant hair
Tamed down,
Patent-leathered now
Until it gleams
Like jet—
Were jet a crown.

The music
From the trumpet at his lips
Is honey
Mixed with liquid fire.
The rhythm
From the trumpet at his lips
Is ecstasy
Distilled from old desire—

Desire
That is longing for the moon

Where the moonlight's but a spotlight
In his eyes,
Desire
That is longing for the sea
Where the sea's a bar-glass
Sucker size.

The Negro
With the trumpet at his lips
Whose jacket
Has a *fine* one-button roll,
Does not know
Upon what riff the music slips
Its hypodermic needle
To his soul—

But softly
As the tune comes from his throat
Trouble
Mellows to a golden note.

Harlem Dance Hall

It had no dignity before.
But when the band began to play,
Suddenly the earth was there,
    And flowers,
    Trees,
    And air,
And like a wave the floor—
That had no dignity before!

Dimout in Harlem

Down the street young Harlem
In the dusk is walking
In the dusky dimout
Down the street is walking

Shadows veil his darkness
Shadows veiling shadows
Soft as dusk the darkness
Veiling shadows cut by laughter
Then a silence over laughter

Shadows veiling silence
Silence veiling shadows
Silence and the shadows
Veiling Harlem's laughter

Silence
No one talking
Down the street young Harlem
In the dark
Is walking.

Motherland

Dream of yesterday
And far-off long tomorrow:
Africa imprisoned
In her bitter sorrow.

Communion

I was trying to figure out
What it was all about
But I could not figure out
What it was all about
So I gave up and went
To take the sacrament
And when I took it
It felt good to shout!

Migration

A little Southern colored child
Comes to a Northern school
And is afraid to play
With the white children.

At first they are nice to him,
But finally they taunt him
And call him "nigger."

The colored children
Hate him, too,
After awhile.

He is a little dark boy
With a round black face
And a white embroidered collar.

Concerning this
Little frightened child
One might make a story
Charting tomorrow.

Stars

O, sweep of stars over Harlem streets,
O, little breath of oblivion that is night.
   A city building
   To a mother's song.
   A city dreaming
   To a lullaby.
Reach up your hand, dark boy, and take a star.
Out of the little breath of oblivion
   That is night,
   Take just
   One star.

Words Like Freedom

Refugee in America

There are words like *Freedom*
Sweet and wonderful to say.
On my heart-strings freedom sings
All day everyday.

There are words like *Liberty*
That almost make me cry.
If you had known what I knew
You would know why.

Earth Song

It's an earth song—
And I've been waiting long
For an earth song.
It's a spring song!
I've been waiting long
For a spring song:
    Strong as the bursting of young buds,
    Strong as the shoots of a new plant,
    Strong as the coming of the first child
    From its mother's womb—
An earth song!
A body song!
A spring song!
And I've been waiting long
For an earth song.

Wisdom

I stand most humbly
Before man's wisdom,
Knowing we are not
Really wise:

If we were
We'd open up the kingdom
And make earth happy
As the dreamed of skies.

Dusk

Wandering in the dusk,
Sometimes
You get lost in the dusk—
And sometimes not.

Beating your fists
Against the wall,
You break your bones
Against the wall—
But sometimes not.

Walls have been known
To fall,
Dusk turn to dawn,
And chains be gone!

When the Armies Passed

Mama, I found this soldier's cap
Lying in the snow.
It has a red star on it.
Whose is it, do you know?
    I do not know
    Whose cap it is, son,
    All stained
    With wet and mud.
But it has a red star on it!
    Are you sure
    It is not blood?
I thought I saw red stars, mother,
Scattered all over the snow.
But if they were blood, mother—
Whose?
    Son, I do not know.
    It might have been
    Your father's blood,
    Perhaps blood
    Of your brother.
See! When you wipe the mud away,
It *is* a red star, mother!

Today

This is earthquake
    Weather!
Honor and Hunger
    Walk lean
    Together.

Oppression

Now dreams
Are not available
To the dreamers,
Nor songs
To the singers.

In some lands
Dark night
And cold steel
Prevail—
But the dream
Will come back,
And the song
Break
Its jail.

Spirituals

Rocks and the firm roots of trees.
The rising shafts of mountains.
Something strong to put my hands on.

  Sing, O Lord Jesus!
  Song is a strong thing.
  I heard my mother singing
  When life hurt her:

Gonna ride in my chariot some day!

  The branches rise
  From the firm roots of trees.
  The mountains rise
  From the solid lap of earth.

The waves rise
From the dead weight of sea.

Sing, O black mother!
Song is a strong thing.

Reprise

Heaven is
The place where
Happiness is
Everywhere.

Animals
And birds sing—
As does
Everything.

To each stone,
"How-do-you-do?"
Stone answers back,
"Well! And you?"

One-Way Ticket

(1949)

To Nathaniel and Geraldine White

Some of these poems first appeared in the following publications, whose editors I thank for permission to reprint: *Poetry, Esquire, Circuit, Tomorrow, The Crisis, Jazz Forum, Opportunity, Negro Story, Ebony Rhythm, Common Ground, Cross-section, The New Yorker, Amsterdam News, Kansas Magazine, Poetry:* Australia, *Contemporary Poetry, Poetry Quarterly:* London, *Seven Poets in Search of an Answer.*

Contents

Madam to You
The Life and Times of Alberta K. Johnson

Madam's Past History

My name is Johnson—
Madam Alberta K.
The Madam stands for business.
I'm smart that way.

I had a
HAIR-DRESSING PARLOR
Before
The depression put
The prices lower.

Then I had a
BARBECUE STAND
Till I got mixed up
With a no-good man.

Cause I had a insurance
The WPA
Said, We can't use you.
Wealthy that way.

I said,
DON'T WORRY 'BOUT ME!
Just like the song,
Take care of yourself—
And I'll get along.

I do cooking,
Day's work, too!

Alberta K. Johnson
Madam to you.

Madam and Her Madam

I worked for a woman,
She wasn't mean—
But she had a twelve-room
House to clean.

Had to get breakfast,
Dinner, and supper, too—
Then take care of her children
When I got through.

Wash, iron, and scrub,
Walk the dog around—
It was too much,
Nearly broke me down.

I said, Madam,
Can it be
You trying to make a
Pack-horse out of me?

She opened her mouth.
She cried, Oh, no!
You know, Alberta,
I love you so!

I said, Madam,
That may be true—
But I'll be dogged
If I love you!

Madam's Calling Cards

I had some cards printed
The other day.
They cost me more
Than I wanted to pay.

I told the man
I wasn't no mint,
But I hankered to see
My name in print.

MADAM JOHNSON,
ALBERTA K.
He said, Your name looks good
Madam'd that way.

Shall I use Old English
Or a Roman letter?
I said, Use American.
American's better.

There's nothing foreign
To my pedigree:
Alberta K. Johnson—
American that's me.

Madam and the Rent Man

The rent man knocked.
He said, Howdy-do?
I said, What
Can I do for you?
He said, You know
Your rent is due.

I said, Listen,
Before I'd pay
I'd go to Hades
And rot away!

The sink is broke,
The water don't run,
And you ain't done a thing
You promised to've done.

Back window's cracked.
Kitchen floor squeaks,
There's rats in the cellar,
And the attic leaks.

He said, Madam,
It's not up to me.
I'm just the agent,
Don't you see?

I said, Naturally,
You pass the buck.
If it's money you want
You're out of luck.

He said, Madam,
I ain't pleased!
I said, Neither am I.

So we agrees!

Madam and the Number Writer

Number runner
Come to my door.
I had swore
I wouldn't play no more.

He said, Madam,
6-0-2
Looks like a likely
Hit for you.

I said, Last night,
I dreamed 7-0-3.
He said, That might
Be a hit for me.

He played a dime,
I played, too,
Then we boxed 'em.
Wouldn't you?

But the number that day
Was 3-2-6—
And we both was in
The *same* old fix.

I said, I swear I
Ain't gonna play no more
Till I get over
To the other shore—

Then I can play
On them golden streets
Where the number not only
Comes out—but repeats!

The runner said, Madam,
That's all very well
But suppose
You goes to hell?

Madam and the Phone Bill

You say I O.K.ed
LONG DISTANCE?
O.K.ed it when?
My goodness, Central,
That was *then!*

I'm mad and disgusted
With that Negro now.
I don't pay no REVERSED
CHARGES nohow.

You say, I will pay it—
Else you'll take out my phone?
You better let
My phone alone.

I didn't ask him
To telephone me.
Roscoe knows darn well
LONG DISTANCE
Ain't free.

If I ever catch him,
Lawd, have pity!
Calling me up
From Kansas City

Just to say he loves me!
I knowed that was so.
Why didn't he tell me some'n
I don't know?

For instance, what can
Them other girls do
That Alberta K. Johnson
Can't do—*and more, too*?

What's that, Central?
You say you don't care
Nothing about my
Private affair?

Well, even less about your
PHONE BILL does I care!

Un-humm-m! . . . Yes!
You say I gave my O.K.?
Well, that O.K. you may keep—

But I *sure* ain't gonna pay!

Madam and the Charity Child

Once I adopted
A little girl child.
She grew up and got ruint,
Nearly drove me wild.

Then I adopted
A little boy.
He used a switch-blade
For a toy.

What makes these charity
Children so bad?
Ain't had no luck
With none I had.

Poor little things,
Born behind the 8-rock,
With parents that don't even
Stop to take stock.

The county won't pay me
But Four a week.
Can't raise no child on that,
So to speak.

And the lady from the
Juvenile Court
Always coming around
Wanting a report.

Last time I told her,
Report, my eye!
Things is bad—
You figure out why!

Madam and the Fortune Teller

Fortune teller looked in my hand.
Fortune teller said,
Madam, It's just good luck
You ain't dead.

Fortune teller squeeze my hand.
She squinted up her eyes.
Fortune teller said,
Madam, you ain't wise.

I said, Please explain to me
What you mean by that?
She said, You must recognize
Where your fortune's at.

I said, Madam, tell me—
For she was *Madam,* too—
Where is my fortune at?
I'll pay some mind to you.

She said, Your fortune, honey,
Lies right in yourself.
You ain't gonna find it
On nobody else's shelf.

I said, What *man* you're talking 'bout?
She said, Madam! Be calm—
For one more dollar and a half,
I'll read your other palm.

Madam and the Wrong Visitor

A man knocked three times.
I never seen him before.
He said, Are you Madam?
I said, What's the score?

He said, I reckon
You don't know my name,
But I've come to call
On you just the same.

I stepped back
Like he had a charm.
He said, I really
Don't mean no harm.

I'm just Old Death
And I thought I might
Pay you a visit
Before night.

He said, You're Johnson—
Madam Alberta K.?
I said, Yes—but *Alberta*
Ain't goin' with you today!

No sooner had I told him
Then I awoke.
The doctor said, Madam,
Your fever's broke—

Nurse, put her on a diet,
And buy her some chicken.
I said, Better buy *two*—
Cause I'm still here kickin'!

Madam and the Minister

Reverend Butler came by
My house last week.
He said, Have you got
A little time to speak?

He said, I am interested
In your soul.
Has it been saved,
Or is your heart stone-cold?

I said, Reverend,
I'll have you know
I was baptized
Long ago.

He said, What have you
Done since then?
I said, None of your
Business, friend.

He said, Sister
Have you back-slid?
I said, it felt good—
If I did!

He said, Sister,
Come time to die,
The Lord will surely
Ask you why!
I'm gonna pray
For you!
Goodbye!

I felt kinder sorry
I talked that way
After Rev. Butler
Went away—
So I ain't in no mood
For sin today.

Madam and Her Might-Have-Been

I had two husbands.
I could of had three—
But my Might-Have-Been
Was too good for me.

When you grow up the hard way
Sometimes you don't know

What's too good to be true,
Just might be so.

He worked all the time,
Spent his money on me—
First time in my life
I had anything free.

I said, Do you love me?
Or am I mistaken?
You're always giving
And never taking.

He said, Madam, I swear
All I want is you.

Right then and there
I knowed we was through!

I told him, Jackson,
You better leave—
You got some'n else
Up your sleeve:

When you think you got bread
It's always a stone—
Nobody loves nobody
For yourself alone.

He said, In me
You've got no trust.

I said, I don't want
My heart to bust.

Madam and the Census Man

The census man,
The day he came round,
Wanted my name
To put it down.

I said, JOHNSON,
ALBERTA K.
But he hated to write
The K that way.

He said, What
Does K stand for?
I said, K—
And nothing more.

He said, I'm gonna put it
K-A-Y.
I said, If you do,
You lie.

My mother christened me
ALBERTA K.
You leave my name
Just that way!

He said, Mrs.,
(With a snort)
Just a K
Makes your name too short.

I said, I don't
Give a damn!
Leave me and my name
Just like I am!

Furthermore, rub out
That MRS., too—
I'll have you know
I'm *Madam* to you!

Life Is Fine

Mama and Daughter

Mama, please brush off my coat.
I'm going down the street.

Where're you going, daughter?

To see my sugar-sweet.

Who is your sugar, honey?
Turn around! I'll brush behind.

He is that young man, mama,
I can't get off my mind.

Daughter, once upon a time—
Let me brush the hem—
Your father, yes, he was the one!
I felt like that about him.

But many a long year ago
He up and went his way—
I hope that wild young son-of-a-gun
Rots in hell today!

Mama, he couldn't be still young.

He *was* young yesterday.
He *was* young when he— Turn around!
So I can brush your back, I say!

S-sss-ss-sh!

Her great adventure ended
As great adventures should
In life being created
Anew—and good.

> *Except the neighbors*
> *And her mother*
> *Did not think it good!*

Nature has a way
Of not caring much
About marriage
Licenses and such.

> *But the neighbors*
> *And her mother*
> *Cared too much!*

The baby came one morning
Almost with the sun.

> *The neighbors*
> *And its grandma*
> *Were outdone!*

Sunday Morning Prophecy

An old Negro minister concludes his sermon in his loudest voice,
having previously pointed out the sins of this world:

. . . and now
When the rumble of death
Rushes down the drain
Pipe of eternity,

And hell breaks out
Into a thousand smiles,
And the devil licks his chops
Preparing to feast on life,
And all the little devils
Get out their bibs
To devour the corrupt bones
Of this world—
Oh-ooo-oo-o!
Then my friends!
Oh, then! Oh, then!
What will you do?

You will turn back
And look toward the mountains.
You will turn back
And grasp for a straw
You will holler,
Lord-d-d-d-ah!
Save me, Lord!
Save me!
And the Lord will say,
In the days of your greatness
I did not hear your voice!
The Lord will say,
In the days of your richness
I did not see your face!
The Lord will say,
No-oooo-ooo-oo-o!
I will not save you now!

And your soul
Will be lost!

Come into the church this morning,
Brothers and Sisters,

And be saved—
And give freely
In the collection basket
That I who am thy shepherd
Might live.

Amen!

Life Is Fine

I went down to the river
I set down on the bank.
I tried to think but couldn't,
So I jumped in and sank.

I came up once and hollered!
I came up twice and cried!
If that water hadn't a-been so cold
I might've sunk and died.

> *But it was*
> *Cold in that water!*
> *It was cold!*

I took the elevator
Sixteen floors above the ground.
I thought about my baby
And thought I would jump down.

I stood there and I hollered.
I stood there and I cried.
If it hadn't a-been so high
I might've jumped and died.

> *But it was*
> *High up there!*

It was high!

Since I'm still here living,
I guess I will live on.
I could've died for love—
But for livin' I was born.

You may hear me holler,
You may see me cry—
But I'll be dogged, sweet baby,
If you gonna see me die.

   Life is fine!
   Fine as wine!
   Life is fine!

Honey Babe

Honey babe,
You braid your hair too tight—
But the good Lord knows
Your heart is right.

I asked you for a dollar.
You gimme two.
That, honey babe,
Is what I like about you.

I knock on your door
About two-three A.M.
You jump out of bed,
Says, *I know it's him!*

There's many another woman
In this wide wide world—

But nary a one
Like my little girl.

Stranger in Town

I walked all over the zoo and the park.
I set down on a stone.
I kept wishing I had a girl-friend
Who would be my very own—
 But I didn't have nary one,
 Not nary one a-tall.

I asked my landlady did I have privileges.
My landlady, she said, No!
I said, It don't make no difference nohow,
Cause I ain't nobody's beau.
 Nobody a-tall—
 I ain't nobody's beau.

Of course, I'm just a stranger
In this strange old town—
But after I been here awhile
I'll know my way around.
 Yes, I'll know
 My way around.

Dark Glasses

Seashore through Dark Glasses

(Atlantic City)

Beige sailors with large noses
Binocular the Atlantic.

At Club Harlem it's eleven
And seven cats go frantic.
Two parties from Philadelphia
Dignify the place
And murmur:

Such Negroes
Disgrace the race!

On Arctic Avenue
Sea food joints
Scent salty-colored
Compass points.

Lincoln Theatre

The head of Lincoln looks down from the wall
While movies echo dramas on the screen.
The head of Lincoln is serenely tall
Above a crowd of black folk, humble, mean.
The movies end. The lights flash gaily on.
The band down in the pit bursts into jazz.
The crowd applauds a plump brown-skin bleached blonde
Who sings the troubles every woman has.

She snaps her fingers, slowly shakes her hips,
And cries, all careless-like from reddened lips!
 De man I loves has
 Gone and done me wrong . . .
While girls who wash rich white folks clothes by day
And sleek-haired boys who deal in love for pay
Press hands together, laughing at her song.

Song for Billie Holiday

What can purge my heart
 Of the song
 And the sadness?
What can purge my heart
 But the song
 Of the sadness?
What can purge my heart
 Of the sadness
 Of the song?

Do not speak of sorrow
With dust in her hair,
Or bits of dust in eyes
A chance wind blows there.
The sorrow that I speak of
Is dusted with despair.

Voice of muted trumpet.
Cold brass in warm air.
Bitter television blurred
By sound that shimmers—
 Where?

Still Here

I've been scarred and battered.
My hopes the wind done scattered.
Snow has frize me, sun has baked me.
    Looks like between 'em
    They done tried to make me
Stop laughin', stop lovin', stop livin'—
    But I don't care!
    I'm still here!

Silhouettes

Blue Bayou

I went walkin'
By de blue bayou
And I saw de sun go down.

I thought about old Greeley
And I thought about Lou
And I saw de sun go down.

    White man
    Makes me work all day
    And I works too hard
    For too little pay—
    Then a white man
    Takes my woman away.

I'll kill old Greeley,

    De blue bayou
    Turns red as fire.
    Put the black man
    On a rope
    And pull him higher!

I saw de sun go down.

    Put him on a rope
    And pull him higher!
    De blue bayou's
    A pool of fire.

And I saw de sun go down,

Down,
    Down!
Lawd, I saw de sun go down!

Flight

Plant your toes in the cool swamp mud.
Step, and leave no track.
Hurry, sweating runner!
The hounds are at your back.

No, I didn't touch her.
White folks ain't for me.

Hurry, black boy, hurry!
Or they'll hang you to a tree!

Silhouette

Southern gentle lady,
Do not swoon.
They've just hung a black man
In the dark of the moon.

They've hung a black man
To a roadside tree
In the dark of the moon
For the world to see
How Dixie protects
Its white womanhood.

Southern gentle lady,
    Be good!
    Be good!

Lynching Song

Pull at the rope!
O, pull it high!
Let the white folks live
And the black boy die.

Pull it, boys,
With a bloody cry.
Let the black boy spin
While the white folks die.

The white folks die?
What do you mean—
The white folks die?

That black boy's
Still body
Says:

NOT I.

One-Way Ticket

One-Way Ticket

I pick up my life
And take it with me
And I put it down in
Chicago, Detroit,
Buffalo, Scranton,
Any place that is
North and East—
And not Dixie.

I pick up my life
And take it on the train
To Los Angeles, Bakersfield,
Seattle, Oakland, Salt Lake,
Any place that is
North and West—
And not South.

I am fed up
With Jim Crow laws,
People who are cruel
And afraid,
Who lynch and run,
Who are scared of me
And me of them.

I pick up my life
And take it away
On a one-way ticket—
Gone up North,
Gone out West,
Gone!

Restrictive Covenants

When I move
Into a neighborhood
Folks fly.

Even every foreigner
That can move, moves.

Why?

The moon doesn't run.
Neither does the sun.

In Chicago
They've got covenants
Restricting me—
Hemmed in
On the South Side,
Can't breathe free.

But the wind blows there.
I reckon the wind
Must care.

Visitors to the Black Belt

You can talk about
Across the railroad tracks—
To me it's *here*
On this side of the tracks.

You can talk about
Up in Harlem—
To me it's *here*
In Harlem.

You can say
Jazz on the South Side—
To me it's hell
On the South Side:

Kitchenettes
With no heat
And garbage
In the halls.

Who're you, outsider?

Ask me who am I.

Juice Joint: Northern City

There is a gin mill on the avenue
Where singing black boys dance and play each night
Until the stars pale and the sky turns blue
And dawn comes down the street all wanly white.
They sell beer foaming there in mug-like cups,
Gin is sold in glasses finger-tall.
Women of the streets stop by for sups
Of whiskey as they start out for a ball.
Sometimes a black boy plays a song
That once was sung beneath the sun
In lazy far-off drowsy Southern days
Before this long hegira had begun
    That brought dark faces
    And gay dancing feet
    Into this gin mill
    On this city street.

Play your guitars, grinning night-dark boys,
And let your songs drift through the swinging doors.

Let your songs hold all the sunny joys
That goad black feet to dancing on bare floors.
Let those women with their lips too red
Turn from the bar and join you in your song,
And switch their skirts and lift their straightened heads
To sing about the men who've done them wrong—
While blues as mellow as the Southern air
And weary as a drowsy Southern rain
Echo the age-less, age-long old despair
That fills a woman's age-less, age-long pain—
    As every swaying
    Guitar-playing boy
    Forgets he ever sang
    A song of joy.

O, in this tavern on the city street
Where black men come to drink and play and sing,
And women, too, whom anyone may meet
And handle easy like a purchased thing,
Where two old brown men stand behind the bar—
Still after hours pouring drinks the law forbids—
Dark dancers dance and dreamers seek a star
And some forget to laugh who still are kids.
But suddenly a guitar-playing lad
Whose languid lean brings back the sunny South
Strikes up a tune all gay and bright and glad
To keep the gall from biting in his mouth,
    Then drowsy as the rain
    Soft sad black feet
    Dance in this juice joint
    On the city street.

Negro Servant

All day subdued, polite,
Kind, thoughtful to the faces that are white.
   O, tribal dance!
   O, drums!
   O, veldt at night!
Forgotten watch-fires on a hill somewhere!
   O, songs that do not care!
At six o'clock, or seven, or eight,
   You're through.
   You've worked all day.
   Dark Harlem waits for you.
   The bus, the sub—
   Pay-nights a taxi
   Through the park.
O, drums of life in Harlem after dark!
   O, dreams!
   O, songs!
   O, saxophones at night!
   O, sweet relief from faces that are white!

Puzzled

Here on the edge of hell
Stands Harlem—
Remembering the old lies,
The old kicks in the back,
The old, *Be patient,*
They told us before.

Sure, we remember.
Now, when the man at the corner store
Says sugar's gone up another two cents,

And bread one,
And there's a new tax on cigarettes—
We remember the job we never had,
Never could get,
And can't have now
Because we're colored.

So we stand here
On the edge of hell
In Harlem
And look out on the world
And wonder
What we're gonna do
In the face of
What we remember.

Who but the Lord?

I looked and I saw
That man they call the law.
He was coming
Down the street at me!
I had visions in my head
Of being laid out cold and dead,
Or else murdered
By the third degree.

I said, *O, Lord, if you can,*
Save me from that man!
Don't let him make a pulp out of me!
But the Lord he was not quick.
The law raised up his stick
And beat the living hell
Out of me!

Now, I do not understand
Why God don't protect a man
From police brutality.
Being poor and black,
I've no weapon to strike back
So who but the Lord
Can protect me?

The Ballad of Margie Polite

If Margie Polite
Had of been white
She might not've cussed
Out the cop that night.

In the lobby
Of the Braddock Hotel
She might not've felt
The urge to raise hell.

A soldier took her part.
He got shot in the back
By a white cop—
The soldier were black.

They killed a colored soldier!
Folks started to cry it—
The cry spread over Harlem
And turned into riot.

They taken Margie to jail
And kept her there.
DISORDERLY CONDUCT
The charges swear.

Margie warn't nobody
Important before—
But she ain't just *nobody*
Now no more.

She started the riots!
Harlemites say
August 1st is
MARGIE'S DAY.

Mark August 1st
As decreed by fate
For Margie and History
To have a date.

Mayor La Guardia
Riding up and down.
Somebody yelled,
*What about
Stuyvesant Town?*

Colored leaders
In sound trucks.
Somebody yelled,
Go home, you hucks!

They didn't kill the soldier,
A race leader cried.
Somebody hollered,
Naw! But they tried!

Margie Polite!
Margie Polite!
Kept the Mayor
And Walter White
And everybody
Up all night!

When the PD car
Taken Margie away—
It wasn't Mother's
Nor Father's—
   It were
MARGIE'S DAY!

Making a Road

Note on Commercial Theatre

You've taken my blues and gone—
You sing 'em on Broadway
And you sing 'em in Hollywood Bowl,
And you mixed 'em up with symphonies
And you fixed 'em
So they don't sound like me.
Yep, you done taken my blues and gone.

You also took my spirituals and gone.
You put me in *Macbeth* and *Carmen Jones*
And all kinds of *Swing Mikados*
And in everything but what's about me—
But someday somebody'll
Stand up and talk about me,
And write about me—
Black and beautiful—
And sing about me,
And put on plays about me!

I reckon it'll be
Me myself!

Yes, it'll be me.

Daybreak in Alabama

When I get to be a composer
I'm gonna write me some music about
Daybreak in Alabama

And I'm gonna put the purtiest songs in it
Rising out of the ground like a swamp mist
And falling out of heaven like soft dew
I'm gonna put some tall tall trees in it
And the scent of pine needles
And the smell of red clay after rain
And long red necks
And poppy colored faces
And big brown arms
And the field daisy eyes
Of black and white black white black people
And I'm gonna put white hands
And black hands and brown and yellow hands
And red clay earth hands in it
Touching everybody with kind fingers
And touching each other natural as dew
In that dawn of music when I
Get to be a composer
And write about daybreak
In Alabama.

Man into Men

A nigger comes home from work:
   Jostle of fur coats
   Jostle of dirty coats
   Jostle of women who shop
   Jostle of women who work
   Jostle of men with good jobs
   Jostle of men in the ditches.

A Negro comes home from work:
   Wondering about fur coats
   Dirty coats

White skins
Black skins
Good jobs
Ditches

A man comes home from work:
Knowing all things
Belong
To the man
Who becomes
Men.

Roland Hayes Beaten

(Georgia: 1942)

Negroes,
Sweet and docile,
Meek, humble, and kind:
Beware the day
They change their minds!

Wind
In the cotton fields,
Gentle breeze:
Beware the hour
It uproots trees!

Democracy

Democracy will not come
Today, this year
Nor ever
Through compromise and fear.

I have as much right
As the other fellow has
    To stand
On my two feet
And own the land.

I tire so of hearing people say,
Let things take their course.
Tomorrow is another day.
I do not need my freedom when I'm dead.
I cannot live on tomorrow's bread.

    Freedom
    Is a strong seed
    Planted
    In a great need.
    I live here, too.
    I want freedom
    Just as you.

October 16

Perhaps
You will remember
John Brown.

John Brown
Who took his gun,
Took twenty-one companions
White and black,
Went to shoot your way to freedom
Where two rivers meet
And the hills of the
North
And the hills of the

South
Look slow at one another—
And died
For your sake.

Now that you are
Many years free,
And the echo of the Civil War
Has passed away,
And Brown himself
Has long been tried at law,
Hanged by the neck,
And buried in the ground—
Since Harpers Ferry
Is alive with ghosts today,
Immortal raiders
Come again to town—

Perhaps
You will recall
John Brown.

Florida Road Workers

Hey, Buddy!
Look at me!

I'm makin' a road
For the cars to fly by on,
Makin' a road
Through the palmetto thicket
For light and civilization
To travel on.

I'm makin' a road
For the rich to sweep over
In their big cars
And leave me standin' here.

Sure,
A road helps everybody!
Rich folks ride—
And I get to see 'em ride.
I ain't never seen nobody
Ride so fine before.

Hey, Buddy! Look!
I'm makin' a road!

Too Blue

Late Last Night

Late last night I
Set on my steps and cried.
Wasn't nobody gone,
Neither had nobody died.

I was cryin'
Cause you broke my heart in two.
You looked at me cross-eyed
And broke my heart in two—

So I was cryin'
On account of
You!

Little Old Letter

It was yesterday morning
I looked in my box for mail.
The letter that I found there
Made me turn right pale.

Just a little old letter,
Wasn't even one page long—
But it made me wish
I was in my grave and gone.

I turned it over,
Not a word writ on the back.

I never felt so lonesome
Since I was born black.

Just a pencil and paper,
You don't need no gun nor knife—
A little old letter
Can take a person's life.

Curious

I can see your house, babe,
But I can't see you.
I can see your house,
But I can't see you.
When you're in your house, baby
Tell me, what do you do?

Bad Morning

Here I sit
With my shoes mismated.
Lawdy-mercy!
I's frustrated!

Lonesome Corner

I went down to the corner.
I stood there feelin' blue—
I used to go *round* the corner,
Babe, and call on you.

Old lonesome corner!
People pass by me—
But none of them peoples
Is who I want to see.

Could Be

Could be Hastings Street,
Or Lenox Avenue,
Could be 18th & Vine
And still be true.

Could be 5th & Mound,
Could be Rampart:
When you pawned my watch
You pawned my heart.

Could be you love me,
Could be that you don't.
Might be that you'll come back,
Like as not you won't.

Hastings Street is weary,
Also Lenox Avenue.
Any place is dreary
Without my watch and you.

Yesterday and Today

O, I wish that yesterday,
Yesterday was today!
Yesterday you was here.
Today you gone away.

I miss you, Lulu,
I miss you so bad—
There ain't no way for me
To get you out of my head.

Yesterday I was happy.
I thought you was happy, too.
I don't know how you feel today—
But, baby, I feel blue.

Too Blue

I got those sad old weary blues.
I don't know where to turn.
I don't know where to go.
Nobody cares about you
When you sink so low.

What shall I do?
What shall I say?
Shall I take a gun
And put myself away?

I wonder if
One bullet would do?
As hard as my head is,
It would probably take two.

But I ain't got
Neither bullet nor gun—
And I'm too blue
To look for one.

Midnight Raffle

Midnight Raffle

I put my nickel
In the raffle of the night.
Somehow that raffle
Didn't turn out right.

I lost my nickel.
I lost my time.
I got back home
Without a dime.

When I dropped that nickel
In the subway slot,
I wouldn't have dropped it,
Knowing what I got.

I could just as well've
Stayed home inside
For my bread wasn't buttered
On neither side.

Monroe's Blues

Monroe's fell on evil days—
His woman and his friend is dead.
Monroe's fell on evil days,
Can't hardly get his bread.

Monroe sings a little blues.
His little blues is sad.

Monroe sings a little blues—
My woman and my friend is dead.

White Felts in Fall

The pimps wear their summer hats
Into late fall
Since the money that comes in
Won't cover it all—
Suit, overcoat, shoes—
And hat, too!

Got to neglect *something*
So what would you do?

Raid

Late at night
When the wine's gone to your head
And the songs on the juke box
Get shorter and shorter,
Baby, say when.

But baby
Doesn't say when.

Suddenly
It's time to go.

Where?

The man is there!

Little Green Tree

It looks like to me
My good-time days done past.
There's nothin' in this world
I reckon's due to last.

I used to play
And I played so dog-gone hard.
Now old age is got me,
Dealt me my bad-luck card.

I look down the road
And I see a little tree.
Little piece down the road
I see a little tree.

Them cool green leaves
Is waitin' to shelter me.

O, little tree!

Blues on a Box

Play your guitar, boy,
Till yesterday's
Black cat
Runs out tomorrow's
Back door
And evil old
Hard luck
Ain't no more!

Home in a Box

Request for Requiems

Play the *St. Louis Blues*
For me when I die.
I want some fine music
Up there in the sky.

Sing the *St. James Infirmary*
When you let me down—
Cause there ain't a good man
Like me left around.

Deceased

Harlem
Sent him home
In a long box—
Too dead
To know why:

The licker
Was lye.

Final Curve

When you turn the corner
And you run into *yourself*
Then you know that you have turned
All the corners that are left.

Boarding House

The graveyard is the
Cheapest boarding house:
   Some of these days
   We'll all board there.
   Rich and poor
   Alike will share.
The graveyard is the
Cheapest boarding house.
   But me—if I can
   Hang on here,
   I ain't gonna
   Go out there.
Let the graveyard be the
Cheapest boarding house!

Funeral

Carried lonely up the aisle
In a box without a smile,
Resting near the altar where
Folks pass by and stare—

   If I was alive
   I'd say,
   I don't give a damn
   Being this-a way!

But I would give a damn.

South Side: Chicago
(A Montage)

Summer Evening
(Calumet Avenue)

Mothers pass,
Sweet watermelon in a baby carriage,
Black seed for eyes
And a rose pink mouth.
Pimps in gray go by,
Boots polished like a Murray head,
Or in reverse
Madam Walker
On their shoe tips.
I. W. Harper
Stops to listen to gospel songs
From a tent at the corner
Where the carnival is Christian.
Jitneys go by
Full of chine bones in dark glasses,
And a blind man plays an accordion
Gurgling *Jericho*.

Theresa Belle Aletha
Throws a toothpick from her window,
And the four bells she's awaiting
Do not ring, not even murmur.
But maybe before midnight
The tamale man will come by,
And if Uncle Mac brings beer
Night will pull its slack taut

And wrap a string around its finger
So as not to forget
That tomorrow is Monday.

A dime on those two bottles.
Yes, they are yours,
Too!

And in another week
It will again
Be Sunday.

Migrant

Daddy-o
Buddy-o
Works at the foundry.
Daddy-o
Buddy-o
Rides the State Street street car,
Transfers to the West Side,
Polish, Bohunk, Irish,
Grabs a load of sunrise
As he rides out on the prairie,
Never knew DuSable,
Has a lunch to carry.

Iron lifting iron
Makes iron of chocolate muscles.
Iron lifting iron
Makes hammer beat of drum beat
And the heat
Moulds and melts and moulds it
On red heart become an anvil
Until a glow is lighted

In the eyes once soft benighted
And the cotton field is frightened
A thousand miles away.

They draw up restrictive covenants
In Australia, too, they say.
Our President
Takes up important matters
Left by V-J Day.
Congress cases Stalin.
The *Tribune*'s hair
Turns gray.

Daddy-o
Buddy-o
Signs his name in uphill letters
On the check that is his pay.
But if he wasn't in a hurry
He wouldn't write so
Bad that way,
Daddy-o.

Graduation

Cinnamon and rayon,
Jet and coconut eyes,
Mary Lulu Jackson
Smooths the skirt
At her thighs.

Mama, portly oven,
Brings remainders from the kitchen
Where the people all are icebergs
Wrapped in checks and wealthy.

Diploma in its new frame:

Mary Lulu Jackson,
Eating chicken,
Tells her mama she's a typist
And the clicking of the keys
Will spell the name
Of a job in a fine office
Far removed from basic oven,
Cookstoves,
And iceberg's kitchen.

Mama says, *Praise Jesus!*
Until then
I'll bring home chicken!

The Diploma bursts its frame
To scatter star-dust in their eyes.

Mama says, *Praise Jesus!*
The colored race will rise!

Mama says,
Praise Jesus!

Then,
Because she's tired,
She sighs.

Third Degree

Hit me! Jab me!
Make me say I did it.
Blood on my sport shirt
And my tan suede shoes.

Faces like jack-o-lanterns
In gray slouch hats.

Slug me! Beat me!
Scream jumps out
Like blow-torch.
Three kicks between the legs
That kill the kids
I'd make tomorrow.

Bars and floor skyrocket
And burst like Roman candles.

When you throw
Cold water on me,
I'll sign the
Paper. . . .

Jitney

Corners
Of South Parkway:
Eeeoooooo!
Cab!
31st,
35th,
39th,
43rd,
Girl, ain't you heard?
No, Martha, I ain't heard.
I got a Chinese boy-friend
Down on 43rd.
47th,
51st,
55th,
63rd,

Martha's got a Japanese!
Child, ain't you heard?
55th,
51st,
47th,
Here's your fare!
Lemme out!
I'm going to the Regal,
See what this week's jive is all about:
The Duke is mellow!
Hibbler's giving out!
43rd,
39th,
Night school!
Gotta get my teaching!
35th,
31st,
Bless God!
Tonight there's preaching!
31st! All out!
Hey, Mister, wait!
I want to get over to State.
I don't turn, Madam!
Understand?
Take a street car
Over to the Grand.

35th,
39th,
43rd,
I quit Alexander!
Honey, ain't you heard?
47th,
50th Place,

63rd,
Alexander's quit Lucy!
Baby, ain't you heard?
Eeeoooooooooo!
Cab!
If you want a good chicken
You have to get there early
And push and shove and grab!
I'm going shopping now, child.
Eeeeooooo!
Cab!
55th,
47th,
35th,
31st,
Hey!
Cab!

Interne at Provident

White coats
White aprons
White dresses
White shoes
Pain and a learning
To take away to Alabama.
Practice on a State Street cancer,
Practice on a stockyards rupture,
Practice on the small appendix
Of 26-girl at the corner,
Learning skills of surgeons
Brown and wonderful with longing
To cure ills of Africa,
Democracy,

And mankind,
Also ills quite common
Among all who stand on two feet.

Brown hands
Black hands
Golden hands in white coat,
Nurses' hands on suture.
Miracle maternity:
Pain on hind legs rising,
Pain tamed and subsiding
Like a mule broke to the halter.

Charity's checked money
Aids triumphant entry squalling
After bitter thrust of bearing
Chocolate and blood:

Projection of a day!

Tears of joy
And Coca-Cola
Twinkle on the rubber gloves
He's wearing.
A crown of sweat
Gleams on his forehead.

In the white moon
Of the amphitheatre
Magi are staring.

The light on the Palmolive Building
Shines like a star in the East.
Nurses turn glass doorknobs
Opening into corridors.

A mist of iodine and ether
Follows the young doctor,
Cellophanes his long stride,
Cellophanes his future.

Uncollected Poems

1941–1950

Addition

7 X 7 + love =
An amount
Infinitely above:
7 X 7 − love.

NAACP

I see by the papers
Where the NAACP
Is meeting down in Houston
And I'd like to be there to see
What they intend to do
In these trying times today
Cause we need to take some solid steps
To drive Jim Crow away.
We need a delegation to
Go see the President
And tell him from the shoulder
Just why we are sent:
Tell him we've heard his speeches
About Democracy—
But to enjoy what he's talking about
What color must you be?
I'm cook or dishwasher in the Navy.
In the Marines I can't be either.
The Army still segregates me—
And we ain't run by Hitler neither!
The Jim Crow car's still dirty.
The color line's still drawn.
Yet up there in Washington
They're blowing freedom's horn!
The NAACP meets in Houston.

Folks, turn out in force!
We got to take some drastic steps
To break old Jim Crow's course.

Watch Out, Papa

When you thrill with joy
At the songs of yesteryear
And declare the ditties
Of today quite drear—
Watch out! You're getting old!

When you extoll the solid
Virtues of *your* youth
And pronounce the young folks
Of *this* age uncouth—
Uh-huh! You're getting old!

Watch Out!
Else you won't know what it's
All about.
Watch Out!

Enemy

It would be nice
In any case,
To someday meet you
Face to face
Walking down
The road to hell . . .
As I come up
Feeling swell.

Refugee

Loneliness terrific beats on my heart,
Bending the bitter broken boughs of pain.
Stunned by the onslaught that tears the sky apart
I stand with unprotected head against the rain.

Loneliness terrific turns to panic and to fear.
I hear my footsteps on the stairs of yesteryear,
Where are you? Oh, where are you?
Once so dear.

It Gives Me Pause

I would like to be a sinner
Sinning just for fun
But I always suffer so
When I get my sinning done.

Some Day

Once more
The guns roar.
Once more
The call goes forth for men.
Again
The war begins,
Again
False slogans become a bore.
Yet no one cries:
ENOUGH! NO MORE!
Like angry dogs the human race
Loves the snarl upon its face

It loves to kill.
The pessimist says
It always will.

That I do not believe.

Some day
The savage in us will wear away.
Some day quite clearly
Men will see
How clean and happy life can be
And how,
Like flowers planted in the sun,
We, too, can give forth blossoms,
Shared by everyone.

Death in Africa

To die
And never know what killed you
When death comes swift
Like a mountain
In the path of a speeding plane
Is O.K. But to die
When death comes slow
Like the tax collector
Year after year
Or the white boss in Africa
Who never goes away,
That's another story.
The drums and the witch doctors, helpless.
The missionaries, helpless.
Damballa,
Helpless, too?

Sunset in Dixie

The sun
Is gonna go down
In Dixie
Some of these days
With such a splash
That everybody who ever knew
What yesterday was
Is gonna forget—
When that sun
Goes down in Dixie.

Gangsters

The gangsters of the world
Are riding high.
It's not the underworld
Of which I speak.
They leave that loot to smaller fry.
Why should they great Capone's
Fallen headpiece seek
When stolen crowns
Sit easier on the head—
Or Ethiopia's band of gold
For higher prices
On the market can be sold—
Or Iraq oil—
Than any vice or bootleg crown of old?
The gangsters of the world ride high—
But not small fry.

Southern Negro Speaks

I reckon they must have
Forgotten about me
When I hear them say they gonna
Save Democracy.
Funny thing about white folks
Wanting to go and fight
Way over in Europe
For freedom and light
When right here in Alabama—
Lord have mercy on me!—
They declare I'm a Fifth Columnist
If I say the word, *Free*.
Jim Crow all around me.
Don't have the right to vote.
Let's leave our neighbor's eye alone
And look after our own mote—
Cause I sure don't understand
What the meaning can be
When folks talk about freedom—
And Jim Crow me?

This Puzzles Me

They think we're simple children:
Watermelon in the sun,
Shooting dice and shouting,
Always having fun.
They think we're simple children,
Grown up never be—
But other simple children
Seem simpler than we.
Other simple children
Play with bombs for toys,
Kill and slaughter every day,
Make a frightful noise,
Strew the world with misery,
Stain the earth with blood,
Slay and maim each other
And evidently think it good—
For when we dark-skinned children
Try to search for right and light
These other simple children
Think it isn't right—
Unless it's white.
Talmadge down in Georgia,
Dies in Washington
Seem to feel that all we need
Is melon in the sun.
They think we're simple children—
Simpler than they—
But why they think it, is a puzzle
When you see the world today.

403 Blues

You lucky to be a spider
Cause it's bad luck to kill you.
Lucky to be a spider.
It's bad luck to kill you.
But if you wasn't a spider
Your day would sure be through.

Evil as I feel this morning
I could whip my weight in lime.
Evil's I feel this morning,
Could whip my weight in lime.
Don't cross my path no mo', spider,
Cause this ain't crossin' time.

Why do you s'pose she left me
Just when I got my 403?
Why do you s'pose my baby left me
When I got my 403?
I reckon, all the time she
Must not of cared for me.

Freedom's Plow

When a man starts out with nothing,
When a man starts out with his hands
Empty, but clean,
When a man starts out to build a world,
He starts first with himself
And the faith that is in his heart—
The strength there,
The will there to build.

First in the heart is the dream.
Then the mind starts seeking a way.
His eyes look out on the world,
On the great wooded world,
On the rich soil of the world,
On the rivers of the world.

The eyes see there materials for building,
See the difficulties, too, and the obstacles.
The hand seeks tools to cut the wood,
To till the soil, and harness the power of the waters.
Then the hand seeks other hands to help,
A community of hands to help—
Thus the dream becomes not one man's dream alone,
But a community dream.
Not my dream alone, but *our* dream.
Not my world alone,
But *your world and my world,*
Belonging to all the hands who build.

A long time ago, but not too long ago,
Ships came from across the sea
Bringing Pilgrims and prayer-makers,
Adventurers and booty seekers,
Free men and indentured servants,
Slave men and slave masters, all new—
To a new world, America!

With billowing sails the galleons came
Bringing men and dreams, women and dreams.
In little bands together,
Heart reaching out to heart,
Hand reaching out to hand,
They began to build our land.
Some were free hands
Seeking a greater freedom,

Some were indentured hands
Hoping to find their freedom,
Some were slave hands
Guarding in their hearts the seed of freedom.
But the word was there always:
    FREEDOM.

Down into the earth went the plow
In the free hands and the slave hands,
In indentured hands and adventurous hands,
Turning the rich soil went the plow in many hands
That planted and harvested the food that fed
And the cotton that clothed America.
Clang against the trees went the ax in many hands
That hewed and shaped the rooftops of America.
Splash into the rivers and the seas went the boat-hulls
That moved and transported America.
Crack went the whips that drove the horses
Across the plains of America.
Free hands and slave hands,
Indentured hands, adventurous hands,
White hands and black hands
Held the plow handles,
Ax handles, hammer handles,
Launched the boats and whipped the horses
That fed and housed and moved America.
Thus together through labor,
All these hands made America.
Labor! Out of labor came the villages
And the towns that grew to cities.
Labor! Out of labor came the rowboats
And the sailboats and the steamboats,
Came the wagons, stage coaches,
Out of labor came the factories,
Came the foundries, came the railroads,

Came the marts and markets, shops and stores,
Came the mighty products moulded, manufactured,
Sold in shops, piled in warehouses,
Shipped the wide world over:
Out of labor—white hands and black hands—
Came the dream, the strength, the will,
And the way to build America.
Now it is Me here, and You there.
Now it's Manhattan, Chicago,
Seattle, New Orleans,
Boston and El Paso—
Now it is the U.S.A.

A long time ago, but not too long ago, a man said:

> ALL MEN ARE CREATED EQUAL . . .
> ENDOWED BY THEIR CREATOR
> WITH CERTAIN INALIENABLE
>   RIGHTS . . .
> AMONG THESE LIFE, LIBERTY
> AND THE PURSUIT OF HAPPINESS.

His name was Jefferson. There were slaves then,
But in their hearts the slaves believed him, too,
And silently took for granted
That what he said was also meant for them.
It was a long time ago,
But not so long ago at that, Lincoln said:

> NO MAN IS GOOD ENOUGH
> TO GOVERN ANOTHER MAN
> WITHOUT THAT OTHER'S CONSENT.

There were slaves then, too,
But in their hearts the slaves knew
What he said must be meant for every human being—

Else it had no meaning for anyone.
Then a man said:

> BETTER TO DIE FREE,
> THAN TO LIVE SLAVES.

He was a colored man who had been a slave
But had run away to freedom.
And the slaves knew
What Frederick Douglass said was true.
With John Brown at Harpers Ferry, Negroes died.
John Brown was hung.
Before the Civil War, days were dark,
And nobody knew for sure
When freedom would triumph.
"Or if it would," thought some.
But others knew it had to triumph.
In those dark days of slavery,
Guarding in their hearts the seed of freedom,
The slaves made up a song:

> KEEP YOUR HAND ON THE PLOW!
>   HOLD ON!

That song meant just what it said: *Hold on!*
Freedom will come!

> KEEP YOUR HAND ON THE PLOW!
>   HOLD ON!

Out of war, it came, bloody and terrible!
But it came!
Some there were, as always,
Who doubted that the war would end right,
That the slaves would be free,
Or that the union would stand.

But now we know how it all came out.
Out of the darkest days for a people and a nation,
We know now how it came out.
There was light when the battle clouds rolled away.
There was a great wooded land,
And men united as a nation.

America is a dream.
The poet says it was promises.
The people say it *is* promises—that will come true.
The people do not always say things out loud,
Nor write them down on paper.
The people often hold
Great thoughts in their deepest hearts
And sometimes only blunderingly express them,
Haltingly and stumbling say them,
And faultily put them into practice.
The people do not always understand each other.
But there is, somewhere there,
Always the *trying* to understand,
And the *trying* to say,
"You are a man. Together we are building our land."

America!
Land created in common,
Dream nourished in common,
Keep your hand on the plow! Hold on!
If the house is not yet finished,
Don't be discouraged, builder!
If the fight is not yet won,
Don't be weary, soldier!
The plan and the pattern is here,
Woven from the beginning
Into the warp and woof of America:

ALL MEN ARE CREATED EQUAL.

NO MAN IS GOOD ENOUGH
TO GOVERN ANOTHER MAN WITHOUT
THAT OTHER'S CONSENT.

BETTER DIE FREE,
THAN LIVE SLAVES.

Who said those things? Americans!
Who owns those words? America!
Who is America? You, me!
We are America!
To the enemy who would conquer us from without,
We say, NO!
To the enemy who would divide
and conquer us from within,
We say, NO!

FREEDOM!
BROTHERHOOD!
DEMOCRACY!

To all the enemies of these great words:
We say, NO!

A long time ago,
An enslaved people heading toward freedom
Made up a song:
　Keep Your Hand On The Plow! Hold On!
That plow plowed a new furrow
Across the field of history.
Into that furrow the freedom seed was dropped.
From that seed a tree grew, is growing, will ever grow.
That tree is for everybody,
For all America, for all the world.
May its branches spread and its shelter grow

Until all races and all peoples know its shade.

    KEEP YOUR HAND ON THE PLOW!
      HOLD ON!

Dear Mr. President

President Roosevelt, you
Are our Commander in Chief.
As such, I appeal
To you for relief.

Respectfully, sir,
I await your reply
As I train here to fight,
Perhaps to die.

I am a soldier
Down in Alabam
Wearing the uniform
Of Uncle Sam.

But when I get on the bus
I have to ride in the back.
Rear seats only
For a man who's black.

When I get on the train,
It's the Jim Crow car—
That don't seem to jibe
With what we're fighting for.

Mr. President, sir,
I don't understand
Democracy that
Forgets the black man.

Respectfully, therefore,
I call your attention
To these Jim Crow laws
Your speeches don't mention.

I ask why YOUR soldiers
Must ride in the back,
Segregated—
Because we are black?

I train to fight,
Perhaps to die.
Urgently, sir,
I await your reply.

Broadcast to the West Indies

Radio Station: Harlem
Wave Length: The Human Heart

    Hello, Jamaica!
    Hello, Haiti!
    Hello, Cuba!
    Hello, Panama!
    Hello, St. Kitts!
    Hello, Bahamas!
All you islands and all you lands
That rim the sun-warmed Carribbean!
Hello! Hello! Hello! Hello!
    I, Harlem,
    Speak to you!

    I, Harlem,
    Island, too.
In the great sea of this day's turmoil.

I, Harlem,
   Little land, too,
Bordered by the sea that washes
   and mingles
With all the other waters of the
   world.

   I, Harlem,
Island within an island, but not
   alone.

   I, Harlem,
Dark-faced, great, enormous
   Negro city
On Manhattan Island, New York,
   U.S.A.

   I, Harlem, say:
   HELLO, WEST INDIES!
You are dark like me,
Colored with many bloods like me,
Verging from the sunrise to the
   dusk like me,
From day to night, from black to
   white like me.
     HELLO! HELLO!
     HELLO, WEST INDIES!

They say—the Axis—
That the U.S.A. is bad:
It lynches Negroes,
Starves them, pushes them aside.
In some states the vote is dead.
Those things are partly true.
They say—the enemy—
Via short wave every day,

That there is now no way
For you to put any faith at all
In what the Yankees say—
They have no love for you
Or any colored people anywhere.
That's also partly true.
There are people here
Who still place greed and power
Above the needs of this most
    crucial hour—
Just as with you there are those
    who place
Imperial will above the needs of
    men.
But here, as there, *their day will
    end.*
Listen, West Indies, they
Are not the U.S.A.

Certain things we know in common:
    Suffering,
    Domination,
    Segregation—
    Locally called
    Jim Crow.

In common certain things we know:
    We are tired!
    Those things
    Must go!

It's a long ways
From where you live to where I
    live—
But there's a direct line
From your heart to mine—

West Indies—Harlem!
Harlem—West Indies!
I like your people, your fruit,
Your sunrise and your song,
Your strength, your sense
Of right and wrong.
We care for each other—

You for me and I for you—
Because we share so much in common,
And because we are aware
Of vast explosions in the air:
    FREEDOM!
    FOR FREEDOM!
    WE PREPARE!
    Hello, West Indies!
    Hello, Jamaica!
    Hello, Haiti!
    Hello, Cuba!
    Hello, Panama!
    Hello, St. Kitts!
    Hello, Bahamas!
    Hello! Hello!
    Hello, West Indies!

Blind

I am blind.
I cannot see.
Color is no bar to me.
I know neither
Black nor white.
I walk in night.
Yet it seems I see mankind

More tortured than the blind.
Can it be that those who know
Sight are often doomed to woe?
Or is it that, seeing,
They never see
With the infinite eyes
Of one like me?

Shall the Good Go Down?

All over the world
Shall the good go down?

Lidice?
Were they good there?
Or did some devil come
To scourge their evil bare?

Shall the good go down?

Who makes fine speeches
Far from the ravaged town?

Spain?
Were folks good there?
Or did some god
Mete punishment
Who did not care?

Who makes fine speeches
Far from the beaten town?

Shall the good go down?

Are we good?
Did we care?

Or did we weary when they said,
Your theme wears bare?
PROPAGANDA—
Boring anywhere.

Shall the good go down?

Who are the good?
Where is their
Town?

Crowing Hen Blues

I was setting on the hen-house steps
When the hen begin to crow.
Setting on the hen-house steps
When the hen begin to crow.
I ain't gonna set on
Them hen-house steps no mo'!

I had a cat, I called him
Battling Tom McCann.
Had a big black cat, I called him
Battling Tom McCann.
Last night that cat riz up and
Started talking like a man.

I said to Baby,
Baby, what do you hear?
I said, Baby,
What on earth do you hear?
Baby said, I don't hear nothin'
But your drunken snorin', dear.

Ummmm-mmm-m-huh! I wish that
Domineck hen wouldn't crow!
Oh-ooo-oo-o, Lawd! Nor that
Black cat talk no mo'!
But, woman, if you don't like it,
Find someplace else to sleep and snore—
Cause I'm gonna drink my licker
Till they burn the licker store.

The Underground

(To the Anti-Fascists of the Occupied
Countries of Europe and Asia.)

Still you bring us with our hands bound,
Our teeth knocked out, our heads broken,
Still you bring us shouting curses,
Or crying, or silent as tomorrow,
Still you bring us to the guillotine,
The shooting wall, the headsman's block.
Or the mass grave in the long trench.

But you can't kill all of us!
You can't silence all of us!
You can't stop all of us!
From Norway to Slovakia, Manchuria to Greece,
We are like those rivers
That fill with the melted snow in spring
And flood the land in all directions.

Our spring will come.

The pent up snows of all the brutal years
Are melting beneath the rising sun of freedom.
The rivers of the world
Will be flooded with strength

And you will be washed away—
You murderers of the people—
You Nazis, Fascists, headsmen,
Appeasers, liars, Quislings,
You will be washed away,
And the land will be fresh and clean again,
Denuded of the past—
For time will give us
Our spring
At last.

Beaumont to Detroit: 1943

Looky here, America
What you done done—
Let things drift
Until the riots come.

Now your policemen
Let your mobs run free.
I reckon you don't care
Nothing about me.

You tell me that hitler
Is a mighty bad man.
I guess he took lessons
From the ku klux klan.

You tell me mussolini's
Got an evil heart.
Well, it mus-a been in Beaumont
That he had his start—

Cause everything that hitler
And mussolini do,

Negroes get the same
Treatment from you.

You jim crowed me
Before hitler rose to power—
And you're STILL jim crowing me
Right now, this very hour.

Yet you say we're fighting
For democracy.
Then why don't democracy
Include me?

I ask you this question
Cause I want to know
How long I got to fight
BOTH HITLER—AND JIM CROW.

Madam and the Army

They put my boy-friend
In 1-A.
But I can't figure out
How he got that way.

He wouldn't work,
Said he wasn't able.
Just drug himself
To the dinner table.

Couldn't get on relief,
Neither WPA.
He wouldn't even try
Cause he slept all day.

I nagged at him
Till I thought he was deaf—
But I never could get him
Above 4-F.

But Uncle Sam
Put him in 1-A
And now has taken
That man away.

If Uncle Sam
Makes him lift a hand,
Uncle's really
A powerful man!

Madam and the Movies

I go to the movies
Once-twice a week.
I love romance.
That's where I'm weak.

But I never could
Understand
Why real life ain't got
No romance-man.

I pay my quarter
And for two hours
Romance reigns
And true love flowers.

Then I come home
And unlock the door—

And there ain't no
Romance any more.

Stalingrad: 1942

There are the inactive ones who,
By their inaction,
Aid in the breaking of your dreams.
There are the ones
Who burn to help you,
But do not know how—
Can only fling words in the air,
Petition: Second Front,
Give money,
Beg, curse, pray,
Bitterly care.

I know—
Those who wreck your dream
Wreck my dream, too,
Reduce my heart to ashes
As they reduce you.

Stalingrad—
Never Paradise—
Just a city on the Volga
Trying peacefully to grow,
A city where some few small dreams
Men dreamt come true.
A simple city
Where all worked, all ate,
All children went to school.
No beggars,
No sick without attention,

No prostitutes,
For women had jobs
And men had wives.
People respected
Each other's lives.
Communal brotherhood,
A city growing toward the good.
Stalingrad—not Paradise—
Yet not bad.

Then out of the West the wreckers came—
Luftwaffe! Panzers! Storm Troopers!
Men with guns and an evil name: Nazis!
Invaders! Bombers! Throwers of flame!
Thieves of the common grain!

   Did we go to help?
     No.
   Did the Second Front open?
     No.
   Did the RAF arrive?
     No.
   Did the AEF get there?
     No.
   Did Stalingrad fall?
   Did Stalingrad fall?
   Did it fall?

Out of the rubble from a dead hand lifted—
Out of the rubble from a lost voice calling—
I gather instead another world is falling:
Lies and blunders and fear and greed
Are meagre feed for the people—
As quick as steel or *ersatz* swill, they kill.

But no one can kill
The dream of men
To be men again.

Beyond the Volga—
Or some more distant stream—
Beyond the desert
Still will live the dream.
In deep hearts
Where now dismayed it lies,
Tomorrow it will rise!

This Hitler understands—
He tries so hard to kill it
Quickly in all lands—
But Stalingrad will rise again,
Rebuilt by hands around the world
That care—as we care—by hands
That grope now in the dark
And don't know why,
Or how to help—but cry
At headlines in the news that say:
STALINGRAD GIVES WAY.

Ethiopia—let it go!
(Retrieved at bloody cost.)
Czechoslovakia—let it go!
    (Lost.)
Spain—let the dogs have it!
India—freedom? The Japs?
They're puzzled at the choice.
(They wait. Too little and too late.)
The same old story—yet today?
The same old patterns—still in power
Even at this hour—as Stalingrad gives way?

Gives way? Oh, no!
Though the last walls fall,
And the last man dies,
And the last bullets go,
Stalingrad does not give way!
Fight on, brave city!
Deathless in song and story,
Yours is the final triumph!

VICTORY—your glory!

Salute to Soviet Armies

Mighty Soviet armies marching on the West,
Red star on your visor, courage on your breast!
Mighty Soviet armies, warriors brave and strong,
Freedom is your watchword as you forge along!
The eyes of all the people, poor upon the earth,
Follow your great battle for mankind's rebirth.
Mighty Soviet armies, allies, comrades, friends,
We will march beside you until fascism ends.

Mighty Soviet armies, guard your fatherland!
The earth of your union warms the hope of man.
Fascist foes surround you with their ring of steel,
But your warriors crush them with a workman's heel.
Never will the people let them rise again.
Death to the fascist tyrants! Death to the Nazi's reign!
Mighty Soviet armies, allies of the free,
We will fight beside you until victory!
Mighty Soviet armies, now as one we stand,
Allies all together for the cause of man!
Salute to the Soviet armies—from our land!

Poem for an Intellectual on the Way Up to Submit to His Lady

Do not call me Dr.
If I get a Ph.D.
Just keep on calling me *Sweetie*
Cause that is good to me.

Do not call me Rev.
If I go into the church.
Address me, *Loving Daddy,*
And my heart will give a lurch.

Don't dare call me Hon.
If I get to be a judge.
Simply call me *Honey Bunch,*
I'll call you *Sugar Fudge.*

I don't believe in titles
When it comes to love,
So, please, do not call me Dr.—
Just call me *Turtle Dove.*

Uncle Tom

Uncle Tom is a legend and a dream.
Uncle Tom is a groan and a scream.
Uncle Tom is a lash on the back.
Uncle Tom is a man who's black.
　　But Uncle Tom
　　Was long ago.
　　Gone is the lash
　　And the slaver's blow.
　　Ours is the freedom
　　Tom did not know—

So tend your freedom that the lash and the pain
And his head bowed down be not in vain.
Tend your freedom that tomorrow may see
Uncle Tom's children wholly free!

Will V-Day Be Me-Day Too?

(A Negro Fighting Man's Letter to America)

Over There,
World War II.

Dear Fellow Americans,
I write this letter
Hoping times will be better
When this war
Is through.
I'm a Tan-skinned Yank
Driving a tank.
I ask, WILL V-DAY
BE ME-DAY, TOO?

I wear a U.S. uniform.
I've done the enemy much harm,
I've driven back
The Germans and the Japs,
From Burma to the Rhine.
On every battle line,
I've dropped defeat
Into the Fascists' laps.

I am a Negro American
Out to defend my land
Army, Navy, Air Corps—
I am there.

I take munitions through,
I fight—or stevedore, too.
I face death the same as you do
Everywhere.

I've seen my buddy lying
Where he fell.
I've watched him dying
I promised him that I would try
To make our land a land
Where his son could be a man—
And there'd be no Jim Crow birds
Left in our sky.

So this is what I want to know:
When we see Victory's glow,
Will you still let old Jim Crow
Hold me back?
When all those foreign folks who've waited—
Italians, Chinese, Danes—are liberated.
Will I still be ill-fated
Because I'm black?

Here in my own, my native land,
Will the Jim Crow laws still stand?
Will Dixie lynch me still
When I return?
Or will you comrades in arms
From the factories and the farms,
Have learned what this war
Was fought for us to learn?

When I take off my uniform,
Will I be safe from harm—
Or will you do me
As the Germans did the Jews?

When I've helped this world to save,
Shall I still be color's slave?
Or will Victory change
Your antiquated views?

You can't say I didn't fight
To smash the Fascists' might.
You can't say I wasn't with you
In each battle.
As a soldier, and a friend.
When this war comes to an end,
Will you herd me in a Jim Crow car
Like cattle?

Or will you stand up like a man
At home and take your stand
For Democracy?
That's all I ask of you.
When we lay the guns away
To celebrate
Our Victory Day
WILL V-DAY BE ME-DAY, TOO?
That's what I want to know.

Sincerely,
GI Joe.

Ennui

It's such a
Bore
Being always
Poor.

Breath of a Rose

Love is like dew
On lilacs at dawn:
Comes the swift sun
And the dew is gone.

Love is like star-light
In the sky at morn:
Star-light that dies
When day is born.

Love is like perfume
In the heart of a rose:
The flower withers,
The perfume goes—

Love is no more
Than the breath of a rose,
No more
Than the breath of a rose.

Moonlight in Valencia: Civil War

Moonlight in Valencia:
The moon meant planes.
The planes meant death.
And not heroic death.
Like death on a poster:
An officer in a pretty uniform
Or a nurse in a clean white dress—
But death with steel in your brain,
Powder burns on your face,
Blood spilling from your entrails,
And you didn't laugh

Because there was no laughter in it.
You didn't cry PROPAGANDA either.
The propaganda was too much
For everybody concerned.
It hurt you to your guts.
It was real
As anything you ever saw
In the movies:
Moonlight. . . .
Me caigo en la ostia!
Bombers over
Valencia.

Madam and the Newsboy

Newsboy knocks,
I buy the DEFENDER.
These colored papers
Is a solid sender.

I read all about
The murdering news,
And who killed who
With the love sick blues.

Then I read
The lynchings and such,
Come to the conclusion
White folks ain't much.

Then I turn over
And read the scandal
In the gossip column,
Initials for a handle.

Then the pictures:
Marva looks well—
But if Joe was my husband,
I'd also look swell.

It's just a matter
Of Who is Who—
If I was Marva I'd be
In the papers, too.
Wouldn't you?

Madam and the Insurance Man

Insurance man,
I heard his knock.
But he couldn't get in
Cause my door was locked.

Week ago Tuesday
He came back agin
This time, I thought,
I'll let him in.

Insurance man said,
It's paying time.
Madam, you are
Six weeks behind.

I said, Mister,
Just let it slumber.
I'll pay in full
When I hit the number.

Insurance man said,
Suppose you die—

Who would bury you?
I said, WHY?

I Dream a World

I dream a world where man
No other man will scorn,
Where love will bless the earth
And peace its paths adorn.
I dream a world where all
Will know sweet freedom's way,
Where greed no longer saps the soul
Nor avarice blights our day.
A world I dream where black or white,
Whatever race you be,
Will share the bounties of the earth
And every man is free,
Where wretchedness will hang its head
And joy, like a pearl,
Attends the needs of all mankind—
Of such I dream, my world!

The Heart of Harlem

The buildings in Harlem are brick and stone
And the streets are long and wide,
But Harlem's much more than these alone,
Harlem is what's inside—
It's a song with a minor refrain,
It's a dream you keep dreaming again.
It's a tear you turn into a smile.
It's the sunrise you know is coming after a while.
It's the shoes that you get half-soled twice.

It's the kid you hope will grow up nice.
It's the hand that's working all day long.
It's a prayer that keeps you going along—
   That's the Heart of Harlem!

It's Joe Louis and Dr. W. E. B.,
A stevedore, a porter, Marian Anderson, and me.
It's Father Divine and the music of Earl Hines,
Adam Powell in Congress, our drivers on bus lines.
It's Dorothy Maynor and it's Billie Holiday,
The lectures at the Schomburg and the Apollo down the way.
It's Father Shelton Bishop and shouting Mother Horne.
It's the Rennie and the Savoy where new dances are born.
It's Canada Lee's penthouse at Five-Fifty-Five.
It's Small's Paradise and Jimmy's little dive.
It's 409 Edgecombe or a cold-water walk-up flat—
But it's where I live and it's where my love is at
   Deep in the Heart of Harlem!

It's the pride all Americans know.
It's the faith God gave us long ago.
It's the strength to make our dreams come true.
It's a feeling warm and friendly given to you.
It's that girl with the rhythmical walk.
It's my boy with the jive in his talk.
It's the man with the muscles of steel.
It's the right to be free a people never will yield.
A dream . . . a song . . . half-soled shoes . . . dancing shoes
A tear . . . a smile . . . the blues . . . sometimes the blues
Mixed with the memory . . . and forgiveness . . . of our wrong.
But more than that, it's freedom—
Guarded for the kids who came along—
   Folks, that's the Heart of Harlem!

Give Us Our Peace

Give us a peace equal to the war
Or else our souls will be unsatisfied,
And we will wonder what we have fought for
And why the many died.

Give us a peace accepting every challenge—
The challenge of the poor, the black, of all denied,
The challenge of the vast colonial world
That long has had so little justice by its side.

Give us a peace that dares us to be wise.
Give us a peace that dares us to be strong.
Give us a peace that dares us still uphold
Throughout the peace our battle against wrong.

Give us a peace that is not cheaply used,
A peace that is no clever scheme,
A people's peace for which men can enthuse,
A peace that brings reality to our dream.

Give us a peace that will produce great schools—
As the war produced great armament,
A peace that will wipe out our slums—
As war wiped out our foes on evil bent.

Give us a peace that will enlist
A mighty army serving human kind,
Not just an army geared to kill,
But trained to help the living mind.

An army trained to shape our common good
And bring about a world of brotherhood.

Harlem Night

Harlem
Knows a song
Without a tune—
The rhythm's there:
But the melody's
Bare.

Harlem
Knows a night
Without a moon.
  The stars
Are where?

Peace Conference in an American Town

At the back fence calling,
    Mrs. Jones!
At the back fence calling,
    Mrs. Greene!
At the back fence calling,
    Mrs. Brown!
    My blueberry pie's
    the best in town.

At the back fence calling,
    Johnny Jones!
At the back fence calling,
    Kenny Greene!
At the back fence calling,
    Buddy Brown!
    Come on, let's
    bat a ball around.

At the back fence calling,
    Neighbor! Neighbor!
At the back fence calling,
    Neighbor! Friend!
At the back fence calling,
    Neighbor! When
    is all this trouble
    gonna end?

At the back fence calling
    Colored, White.
At the back fence calling
    Gentile, Jew.
At the back fence calling
    Neighbor!

At the back fence calling
    You!

Labor Storm

Now it is time
For the strike-breakers to come out:
The boys with the shifting eyes,
The morons,
The discriminated ones
Too bitter to understand,
The goons,
The gangsters of defeat and death,
The strong-armed mercenaries
With the alley breath.

Now it is time for the worms
To come out of their holes,
And the little snakes

Who wrap themselves around
The big snakes,
Time for the white bellied things
To bare their atavistic fangs
For dollars and gray shame.

Man knows well
The use of man against men,
The greedy few
Against the needy many,
The decayed against the healthy,
The snakes
Against the runners in the sun.

Too often in the past
The snakes have won.

Time now that men awake
To their old past mistake
Of trust in snakes
Who wear a tailored skin—
But when in trouble
Call less stylish vipers in,
Moccasins that strike
The unprotected heel of hunger
Without shame—
Since no great respected firm
Bears that anonymous name:
STRIKEBREAKER—
At least, not on the door.

The storm
That calls up varmints
From the earth
Is coming.

Workers beware!
It's almost
Here!

Lenin

Lenin walks around the world.
Frontiers cannot bar him.
Neither barracks nor barricades impede.
Nor does barbed wire scar him.

Lenin walks around the world.
Black, brown, and white receive him.
Language is no barrier.
The strangest tongues believe him.

Lenin walks around the world.
The sun sets like a scar.
Between the darkness and the dawn
There rises a red star.

First of May

I believe it to be true,
You see,
Tomorrow
Now belongs to me—
And so
Let not too many tears
Water these unhappy years.
Being poor and black today,
I await
My first of May.

Conservatory Student Struggles with Higher Instrumentation

The saxophone
Has a vulgar tone.
I wish it would
Let me alone.

The saxophone
Is ordinary.
More than that,
It's mercenary!

The saxophone's
An instrument
By which I wish
I'd never been
Sent!

Comment

Spiral Death
The snake must be—
Yet he's never
Murdered me.

Fanged death
The tiger, too—
But has he ever
Murdered you?

More dangerous death
Man indeed
Who often kills
When there's no need.

For man will kill
Animal—or you—
For strife, for sport,
Or just a stew.

To Dorothy Maynor

As though her lips
Are touched
With cooling water
The calmness of her song
Is blessed
With peace.

Barefoot Blues

Papa, don't you see my shoes?
Papa, don't you see my shoes?
   What you want
   Yo' little boy to do,
   Keep on goin' round
   Feelin' blue?
Walkin' with them barefoot blues.

Papa, don't you see my feet?
Looky, don't you see my feet?
   How you want
   Yo' sugar-lump to walk,
   Pattin' leather
   On the street?

Papa, is yo' money gone?
Tell me, is yo' money gone?

I'm as cold
As cold can be!
What you gonna do
'Bout these shoes and me?
Papa, is your money gone?

Wealth

From Christ to Gandhi
Appears this truth—
St. Francis of Assisi
Proves it, too:
Goodness becomes grandeur
Surpassing might of kings.
Halos of kindness
Brighter shine
Than crowns of gold,
And brighter
Than rich diamonds
Sparkles
The simple dew
Of love.

Wisdom and War

We do not care—
That much is clear.
Not enough
Of us care
Anywhere.

We are not wise—
For that reason,

Mankind dies.

To think
Is much against
The will.

Better—
And easier—
To kill.

From Selma

In places like
Selma, Alabama,
Kids say,
    In places like
    Chicago and New York. . . .
In places like
Chicago and New York
Kids say,
    In places like
    London and Paris. . . .
In places like
London and Paris
Kids say,
    In places like
    Chicago and New York. . . .

Ballad of the Seven Songs
A Poem for Emancipation Day

Seven letters,
Seven songs.

The seven letters
F-R-E-E-D-O-M
Spell *Freedom*.
The seven songs
Capture segments of its history
In terms of black America.

Seven songs,
Seven names:
    Cudjoe
    Sojourner Truth
    Harriet Tubman
    Frederick Douglass
    Booker T. Washington
    Dr. Carver
    Jackie
Seven men and women
From unrecorded slavery to recorded free:

For Emancipation Day
Seven songs,
Seven men,
Seven letters
That spell *Freedom*.

It was an easy name to give a slave
So they called him Cudjoe.
There were four million Cudjoes
Before Emancipation came.

What did it mean to be a slave?
That you could not choose your own son's name,
Nor your own son's father or mother,
Nor your own son's home, or work, or way of life,
(Nor indeed could you choose your own)
Nor choose to have or not have a son.

No part of life or self
Belonged to Cudjoe—slave.

To Cudjoe—slave—
Only a dream belonged.
Seven letters spelled the dream:
F-R-E-E-D-O-M
Freedom!
But in the cane fields, in the rice fields,
In the bondage of the cotton,
In the deep dark of the captive heart
Sometimes Freedom seemed so far away,
Farther away than the farthermost star,
So far, so far—
That only over Jordan was there a dream
Called Freedom.
Cudjoe's song was:
  Deep river,
  My home is over Jordan.
  Deep river, Lord,
  I want to cross over into camp ground.
  O, don't you want to go to that gospel feast,
  That promised land where all is peace? . . .
  Deep river, Lord,
  I want to cross over into camp ground.

Death was a deep river,
And only over Jordan, Freedom.
Oh, night! Oh, moon! Oh, stars!
Oh, stars that guide lone sailing boats
Across the great dark sea,
Star, guide thou me!

Star! Star! Star!
North Star! North.
I cannot catch my breath

For fear of that one star
And that one word:
Star—Free—Freedom—North Star!
Where is the road that leads me to that star?
Ah, ha! The road?
Dogs guard that road,
Patrollers guard that road,
Bloodhounds with dripping muzzles
Guard that road!
Gun, lash, and noose
Guard that road!

Freedom was not a word:
Freedom was the dark swamp crossed,
And death defied,
Fear laid aside,
And a song that whispered, crooned,
And while it whispered cried:

> *Oh, Freedom!*
> *Freedom over me!*
> *Before I'd be a slave,*
> *I'd be buried in my grave*
> *And go home to my Lord*
> *And be free!*

Harriet Tubman—slave.
She wanted to be free.
She'd heard of that word with seven letters.
She could not read the word,
Nor spell the word,
But she smelled the word,
Tasted the word,
On the North wind heard the word.
And she saw it in a star.

Before I'd be a slave,
I'd be buried in my grave
And go home to my Lord
And be free!

Sojourner Truth—slave.
She wanted to be free.
Her sons and daughters sold away,
Still she wanted to be free.
She said:

    I look up at de stars,
    My chillun look up at de stars.
    They don't know where I be
    And I don't know where they be.
    God said, Sojourner, go free!
Go free! Free! Freedom! Free!

Before I'd be a slave
I'd be buried in my grave. . . .

Before Emancipation thousands of slaves
Made their way to freedom—
Through swamp and brier, over field and hill,
By dark of night, prayer-guided, star-guided,
Guided by that human will that makes men love
A word called Freedom—
And the deep river was not Jordan, but the Ohio,
Home was not heaven, but the North.
North! North Star! North!

Frederick Douglass called his paper
"The North Star."

Douglass had made his way to freedom.
Sojourner Truth made her way to freedom.
Harriet Tubman made her way to freedom;

Then she went back into slavery land,
And back again, and back again, and again, again,
Each time bringing a band of slaves
(Who once were slaves, now slaves no more)
To freedom!
Before the Civil War,
Long before '61,
Before Emancipation,
Freedom had begun!

> *Go down, Moses,*
> *Way down in Egypt land*
> *Tell old Pharaoh*
> *To let my people go!*

Linking arms for freedom
With the one-time slaves,
With Douglass, Harriet, Sojourner,
Were Whittier, Garrison, Lovejoy, Lowell—
Great Americans who believed in all men being free.
And thousands more—white, too, but not so famous—
Dared arrest and scorn and persecution
That black men might be free:
The stations of the underground railroad to freedom
Became many—
And the North Star found a million friends.
And of that time a book was born, "Uncle Tom's Cabin."
And a spirit was born, John Brown.
And a song was born:

> *Mine eyes have seen the glory of the coming of the Lord:*
> *He is trampling out the vintage where the grapes of wrath are stored;*
> *He hath loosed the fateful lightning of his terrible swift sword. . . .*

And a war was born:

John Brown's body lies
A-mouldering in the grave—
But his soul goes marching on!

And a voice to set the nation right:

With malice toward none,
With charity for all. . . .

Lincoln . . .

In the beauty of the lilies Christ was born across the sea,

Abraham . . .

With a glory in His bosom that transfigures you and me;

Lincoln . . .

As he died to make men holy, let us die to make men free,

Abraham . . .

While God is marching on.

Lincoln . . .

In giving freedom to the slave
we assure freedom to the free. . . .

Abraham . . .

No man is good enough to govern another
man without that other's consent.

Lincoln . . .

I do ordain . . . thenceforward and forever free.

But the fields still needed planting,

The cane still needed cutting,
The cotton still needed picking,
The old mule still needed a hand to guide the plow:

 De cotton needs pickin'
 So bad, so bad, so bad!
 De cotton needs pickin' so bad!
 Gonna glean all over this field!

And on the river boats the song:

 Roll dat bale, boy!
 Roll dat bale! . . .

Up the river to Memphis, Cairo, St. Louis,
Work and song, work and song—stevedores, foundry men,
Brick layers, builders, makers, section hands, railroad shakers:

 There ain't no hammer
 In this mountain
 Rings like mine, boys,
 Rings like mine!

Freedom is a mighty word,
But not an easy word.
You have to hold hard to freedom.
And as somebody said,
Maybe you have to win it all over again every generation.
There are no color lines in freedom.
But not all the "free" are free.
Still it's a long step from Cudjoe—slave,
From Harriet Tubman—slave,
Sojourner Truth—slave
Frederick Douglass—slave
Who had to run away to freedom—
It's a long step to Booker T. Washington
Building Tuskegee,

To Dr. W. E. B. Du Bois building a culture for America.
It's a long step from Cudjoe—slave
Hoeing cotton—
To George Washington Carver—once slave—
Giving his discoveries in agricultural chemistry to the world. It's a long
song from:

> *Before I'd be a slave*
> *I'd be buried in my grave. . . .*

To Dorothy Maynor singing, "*Depuis le jour.*"
It's a long step from Cudjoe—slave—
To Jackie Robinson hitting a homer.

Yet to some Freedom is still
Only a part of a word:
Some of the letters are missing.
Yet it's enough of a word
To lay hands on and hope,
It's enough of a word
To be a universal star—
Not just a North Star anymore:

Thenceforward and forever—free!

> *Oh, Freedom!*
> *Freedom over me!*
> *Before I'd be a slave*
> *I'd be buried in my grave*
> *And go home to my Lord*
> *And be free!*

Dare

Let darkness
Gather up its roses
Cupping softness
In the hand—
Till the hard fist
Of sunshine
Dares the dark
To stand.

Slave Song

I can see down there
That star that brings no peace—
I can see in the East
It does shine.

I can see in the West
The star that does not care—
But the star in the North
  Is mine!

  Guiding star!
  Wishing star!
  North star!

  How far?

Second Generation: New York

Mama
Remembers the four-leaf clover
And the bright blue Irish sky.

I
Remember the East River Parkway
And the tug boats passing by.

I
Remember Third Avenue
And the el trains overhead,
And our one window sill geranium
Blooming red.

Mama
Remembers Ireland.
All I remember is here—
And it's dear!

Papa
Remembers Poland,
Sleighs in the wintertime,
Tall snow-covered fir trees,
And faces frosty with rime.

Papa
Remembers pogroms
And the ghetto's ugly days.
I remember Vocational High,
Park concerts,
Theatre Guild plays.

Papa
Remembers Poland.
All I remember is here—
   This house,
   This street,
   This city—
And they're dear!

Homecoming

I went back in the alley
And I opened up my door.
All her clothes was gone:
She wasn't home no more.

I pulled back the covers,
I made down the bed.
A *whole* lot of room
Was the only thing I had.

From Spain to Alabama

Where have the people gone
That they do not sing
Their *flamencos?*

The people
Have gone nowhere:
They still sing
Their flamencos.

Where have the people gone
That they do not sing
Their blues?

The people
Have gone nowhere:
They still sing
Their blues.

To Be Somebody

Little girl
Dreaming of a baby grand piano
(Not knowing there's a Steinway bigger, bigger)
Dreaming of a baby grand to play
That stretches paddle-tailed across the floor,
Not standing upright
Like a bad boy in the corner,
But sending music
Up the stairs and down the stairs
And out the door
To confound even Hazel Scott
Who might be passing!

Oh!

Little boy
Dreaming of the boxing gloves
Joe Louis wore,
The gloves that sent
Two dozen men to the floor.
Knockout!
Bam! Bop! Mop!

There's always room,
They say,
At the top.

Catch

Big Boy came
Carrying a mermaid
On his shoulders
And the mermaid

Had her tail
Curved
Beneath his arm.

Being a fisher boy,
He'd found a fish
To carry—
Half fish,
Half girl
To marry.

Island

Wave of sorrow,
Do not drown me now:

I see the island
Still ahead somehow.

I see the island
And its sands are fair:

Wave of sorrow,
Take me there.

Kid in the Park

Lonely little question mark
on a bench in the park:

See the people passing by?
See the airplanes in the sky?
See the birds
flying home

before
dark?

Home's just around
the corner
there—
*but not really
anywhere.*

Index of First Lines

Index of Titles